LEARN TO PLAY THE

ROCK
STEADY

How your child can grow
in confidence, develop life skills
and have fun learning music

WAY

MARK ROBINSON

To my parents,
who made anything possible.

CONTENTS

INTRODUCTION

'What do you do?'

It's a question we all get asked when we meet new people.

For me, the answer is this: having started a company called Rocksteady Music School, I'm now responsible for nurturing its growth and development.

And what's Rocksteady all about?

The simple answer is that we teach primary school children aged four to eleven to play in bands from the first time they pick up an instrument They form a band with their peers, learn songs that they love, and work towards playing concerts for their fans. To start with that means family and friends, just like it does for a 'real' band. It's great for children because it's fun, it builds their musical ability in ways that traditional lessons don't, and it's a game changer for their confidence.

'That's exciting!' is the usual reply. It's never hard to start a conversation about what Rocksteady does, because it is exciting for most people. Take a child at an age when they're full of potential and give them the opportunity to express themselves in this way, and truly brilliant things can happen.

But that doesn't tell you why we're so passionate about it or why we believe it's important. It says little about how we came across this method of teaching, and how it evolved from a blizzard of trial and error, U-turns and interesting experiments.

It doesn't really tell you about what it can do for children. About how learning music in the right way builds the whole child, not just their musical ability.

In this book, I'll be sharing these things, and more, with you.

Building the whole child has always been at the heart of what we do. The way we do that has been guided by experience, philosophies on education and teaching music; and there are thousands of children, parents, musicians and school teachers who have helped to form what the business is today. From the start, we listened hard to what *everyone* was telling us. What worked about music lessons and what didn't? What were the children excited by? Why did they want to learn music in the first place? What built them up? And just as importantly, what would knock them down? Children may not be able to articulate exactly what music education should look like, but they're not at all shy in telling anybody what motivates them or what they think about a lesson. It's all there if you listen carefully enough.

In many cases, traditional music lessons have been missing out on the essence of music. They have reduced the collective spirit and emotional engagement of an exciting art form into a set of skills to be learned and demonstrated in exams. They've put a lot of children off learning it and failed to share all the other wonderful benefits music can bring.

This book is about changing that for the better, and why it's important for us to do so.

It's also about the different roles music plays in children's lives. For some, it takes centre stage and becomes a guiding star. For others, it simply makes them very happy to be able to play songs they love and share them with their friends. Music can play a supporting role that helps to build confidence and, as we are experimenting with now, it can also develop children's independence. In this book, we'll be looking at all of these possibilities through the eyes of the children, parents and teachers who are on the journey together. We'll be covering:

Why music is important, what happens for children in a traditional music lesson and why we decided to do it differently

How children feel about learning music and why it's imperative that we put this at the centre of how we teach them

The core principles of teaching children music today, from how to teach music as a language to how to spot the right tutor for your child.

The Rocksteady method, what it does well and why it works, from first band rehearsals and concerts to developing children into independent, self-confident musicians.

It is written largely for the benefit of parents who have children in music lessons or are considering introducing them to music, which is why you will often find references to 'your child'. There are tips on how you can help at home littered throughout, and specifically in Chapter 8. However, the principles within apply equally to classroom teachers at primary school, head teachers and music tutors who are interested in developing their teaching. I believe that together, we have a joint responsibility in giving music and its wider benefits to the next generation.

I also believe that learning to play music should be for everyone, not just those who have an exceptional aptitude for it. It's important for us to continue to work on making all aspects of education as accessible as possible for all children. Music is no exception.

I hope that you find this book an interesting read and that it helps you to support children in playing music – or whatever it is that they're passionate about doing.

Best wishes

Mark Robinson
Rocksteady Music School.

PART 1
ROCKSTEADY ROOTS

In this section we'll be looking at why learning to play music can be an important part of your child's life. In Chapter 1, we'll learn what it feels like to be a child performing in front of an audience, whether it's friends and family or thousands of people, and how it can be a life-affirming, empowering experience.

In Chapter 2 we'll cover how learning an instrument in the traditional way can be discouraging to some children, and why practice and exams are used as carrots and sticks, raising the question of whether they are a good idea in the long run.

In Chapter 3 I'll be telling my own story – what motivated me to get into music and how the Rocksteady method was inspired by a desire to make a change for the next generation, aided by some wonderful parents, teachers and children who were prepared to give something new a try.

WHY THIS IS IMPORTANT

It's 5pm, 1 July 2015, and it's a typical British summer day. Warm and cloudy. In a dressing room backstage at the Guildhall in Portsmouth, there are thirteen musicians getting ready to play the concert of their lives. The group is made up of two bands: Louis, Jack B, Lucas, Jacob, Kieran and Jack C belong to the Lightning Beasts, and Ben, Leila, James, Kyra, Thomas, Jack S and Tianna form Leopard Clone Wars.

They'll be playing to a crowd of around 2,000 people tonight, and they're currently warming up by strumming on unplugged instruments and drumming on the table. The usual pre-gig nerves are there. Jack, the Lightning Beasts' drummer, describes butterflies dancing in his stomach. Some deal with their nerves by becoming quiet and withdrawn, others by being loud and cracking jokes at every opportunity.

Ten minutes to go until the show starts. The feeling of energy building in this cramped, hot room is immense. You can feel it bouncing off the walls.

Over the last fifty years, many bands have occupied that space at the Guildhall waiting to go on and play. As one of the South's biggest venues, it attracts some huge names, ranging from McFly to Motörhead, and just about everything in between. Many bands have doubtless felt the same excited, nervous energy about stepping on stage, and the immense physical and psychological rush when they connect to an auditorium full of equally excited people there to hear them play.

What sets our bands apart from these others is that the Lightning Beasts are all between nine and ten years old, and the Leopard Clone Wars have just turned six. It's both bands' first time playing in front of this many people, and they're going to be covering 'Firework' by Katy Perry and 'Steal My Girl' by One Direction: songs they've chosen and have been rehearsing at school for the last ten weeks.

'How Many People Are Watching Me?'

Their ten minutes' waiting is up, and the first of the bands to go on is Leopard Clone Wars. Their logo (which they designed) is blown up to at least 10 feet tall and projected on to the back of the stage, then their name is called.

Thomas, one of the more boisterous band members, looks up at me with wild eyes.

'How many people are going to be watching me?'

'Thousands!' I smile. Before he knows what's happened, he's on stage behind the keyboard, the lights are down and he's focused. The crowd's cheers have died down and the band instinctively feels it's time to start. Their tutor, Luke, gives them the nod. This is going to be awesome.

Their drummer Ben clicks in 'One, two, three, four' and off they go. The keyboard chords swell softly, creating a gentle ambience for the introduction. The guitarists and bass player are playing sparsely but at exactly the right time, and it's all being held together by Ben's driving rhythm on the drums. A relentless time keeper, he taps away at the cymbal to let the rest of the band know where the beat is. And they're listening intently. After a couple of rounds of the chord sequence, Tianna puts her lips to the microphone and sings the opening lines.

The unmistakable sound of a young child singing their heart out: it can't fail to make you smile. We've all heard it, but rarely in this context. As they build towards the chorus with more notes, crash cymbals and dynamics coming into play, I look out over the audience from the side of the stage. They can't quite believe what they're seeing. This is 'Firework', a recognisable song, being played well by a band who are all knee high to a grasshopper. What's more, they look like they're having the time of their lives.

If you had asked me five years ago whether a band of six-year-olds could get up on stage and play a famous pop song independently, I wouldn't have believed it either. Now, it was happening right in front of me.

The band finishes with a crash and the crowd break into a cheer. It's smiles all round, from ear to ear: the parents, the children on stage, and especially their tutor Luke.

'What Happens If I Make A Mistake?'

The smiles continue as the children leave the stage and the Lightning Beasts step up to the plate. They're just four years older than the previous band, but the difference is noticeable. With an average age of ten, they're far more self-aware and have a much better understanding of what it means to put yourself out there in front of people. Especially if you're singing.

The Lightning Beasts' guitarist and lead singer Lucas has been one of the quiet ones back stage. While his band mates have been busy burning up their energy bouncing off the walls, Lucas had been sitting quietly, going over things in his mind.

'What happens if I make a mistake or sing the wrong words?' he asks.

'It's okay, nobody will notice,' I tell him.

'Are you sure? Even if I sing completely the wrong words? I did that once when we were filming our rehearsal.'

'It'll be okay,' I reassure him. 'How many mistakes do you think I make when I play a concert?'

'None,' he offers, innocently.

'Guess again, it's hundreds. The audience don't mind. They care more that you're making good music for them and having a good time with them.'

Lucas looks sceptical but nods thoughtfully.

Now they're on stage and the spotlight is shining squarely on him. The band play a solid intro and the music fades to give space for Lucas to sing his first line. He looks down at his guitar, steps up to the microphone and delivers it with confidence.

The crowd don't save their encouragement for the end this time: they erupt with applause, whistles and cheers right from the start. Lucas smiles; the rest of the band smile. They relax into it, start moving with their instruments and put on a great show for the crowd. There are build-ups, dropdowns, drum fills, keyboard riffs and backing vocals. Everything you would expect from an exciting band doing their thing. After a big final chorus, there's a rock ending full of crashes, furious guitar strumming and an excited crowd cheering over the top. They play their final note and take a second to appreciate what just happened before bouncing off the stage.

Jack B, the drummer, is the first to speak. 'I wanna go back and do that again!' he says, eyes beaming.

I know exactly what he means. It's a feeling that many musicians can relate to. It's the feeling that takes us back to the rehearsal room to work hard on our craft. It's the feeling that pulls us back to the stage time and time again to play for other people. The stage is where we feel happy and engaged. It's a place to express ourselves and share it with others. It's where we feel alive. I've experienced it; Jack's just experienced it. But you don't have to be playing in front of thousands to reap the benefits.

April 1 2015:
Holly Spring Infant School, Bracknell

Three months earlier, it was the first Rocksteady concert at Holly Spring Infant School in Bracknell. The children had been learning since January and this was their first opportunity to play in front of their school friends and parents.

What's more, it was also their tutor Josh's first concert with the company.

The children were all aged between four and seven. I sat at the back of the room with the parents as the other schoolchildren filed into the hall. Nobody knew quite what to expect, but the buzz and excitement you would associate with any gig was definitely there.

A parent leaned back from the row in front of me to have a chat.

'My son's been doing this since you started in January and he never stops talking about it! He's so excited about today, he's been up since six drumming away on the kitchen table.'

You would think from this that her son had been learning the drums, but he was actually going to play guitar for us today.

'He doesn't have a guitar at home,' she explained, 'but he's started tapping on everything and calling out notes.'

One of the nice things about playing in a band rather than on your own is you become very aware of what the other band members are doing and how your part fits into it. Although you may play guitar, you know that it only counts if your notes are in time with the drummer. Even without an instrument at home, our young guitarist was rehearsing his part so it fitted in with everyone else's.

The head teacher gave a nice introduction, saying how we were going to see what the children had been learning with Rocksteady over the last term. Today we were going to hear from the Velociraptors, Strike A Beat, the Rock Dragons and the Blue Wolves. Four bands, twenty-five children and four modern pop songs.

First up was the Velociraptors, a band of Year R and Year 1 children playing 'Best Day of My Life' by American Authors. Their tutor Josh had done a great job of helping them pick the right song as it only has two chords and a very simple beat. Each band member had two things to remember. For the drummer it was hit the right drum or hit both drums. For guitarists and keyboard players it was a D and a G. The singer just had to remember the chorus, which consisted of 'Wo-oh-oh-oh-oh's and the line 'This is gonna be the best day of my life', and sing it eight times.

They had all learned their parts and could play them well enough. The challenge was going to be playing them at the right time, and in a band that means in time with each other. What's even more challenging is doing this when you're standing in front of your entire peer group, teachers and parents and you're excited, scared and trying to concentrate all at the same time. But they did a remarkable job.

After a few rounds to get into the swing of things, Josh signalled for the singer to come in. Everyone in the room recognised the song and started singing along. Eight rounds later, the Velociraptors finished at (roughly!) the same time and received a well-deserved round of applause from their friends and family.

We then saw three more performances of songs from the charts. All simplified, but all very recognisable. The highlight for many of the teachers in the room was six-year-old Maya singing 'Price Tag' by Jessie J, rap included.

The concert at Holly Spring was on a much smaller scale than the Guildhall, but no less significant to the children and parents involved. For the children, playing music they were excited about to a crowd of people brought the same feelings of joy. For the parents, seeing their children get up and do something fun in front of others made them feel immensely proud. There's little more satisfying than watching your child grow in confidence before your very eyes.

Rocksteady Principles

That same week, similar scenes played out in 100 schools across the South of England. There were just over 500 bands performing involving nearly 3,000 children, the large majority of whom had learned to play their instruments using the Rocksteady method.

This meant that they learned to play in a band from day one, decided as a group what to call themselves and worked with their tutors (who we call band leaders) to figure out what song they should play. They would be building their knowledge of different notes, rhythms and techniques naturally over time as a need for them came up, much like they had learned to speak. Scales, sight reading and tongue-twisting Italian names for basic words like fast and slow didn't belong at this party. The children knew that they were working towards playing a concert to their friends and family and would be responsible for playing their part. Playing in a band is a team sport, even for those who don't like sports.

They would be playing covers of rock, pop, dance, Disney songs – you name it, it was in there. For some it meant showcasing their own songs. For some it was their first concert, for others their twentieth.

There were loud kids, shy kids, excited kids, helpful kids, serious kids, determined kids, kids who couldn't (and still can't) sit still. There were logos designed, arguments (we call them heated discussions) about who was going to play bass on this gig, team hugs, break ups and make ups. There were boys, girls, younger, older, beginners, experienced. They all had a part to play, and they were learning about far more than just how to play their instruments in the process.

The Value Of Music

Music is a wonderful thing. Like most art forms, if you boil it down to its core, it's about communication. Communication is fundamental to who we are as humans; it's allowed us to work together, build societies and face all sorts of adversity. It's also allowed us to empathise with one another and express our feelings healthily. Through music, you can communicate among a group of people for the enjoyment of both the musicians and the audience. Music moves us to feel many shades of happiness, sorrow, surprise and even fear. And we enjoy feeling all of them, because music gives us a safe space in which to experience these emotions.

To be able to make music with other people, you need to develop high level listening skills, teamwork, co-operation and resilience. To be able to play it for other people, you need concentration and confidence, not to mention a healthy dose of bravery. These skills and qualities can take you a long way in life.

And the great thing about it is anyone and everyone can do it. That's right, *anyone* can learn to play an instrument and gain the substantial benefits it brings. Not everyone might want to, but the point is that everyone can.

But not all music lessons acknowledge why we make music in the first place. Even fewer attempt to reap the full benefits and build the whole person in this manner. Think back to your music lessons at school. Were they fun and engaging? Did you look forward to them each week and play enthusiastically when you got home? Was your teacher a role model for you?

If you answered yes to these questions, then you were one of the lucky ones. Does dry, repeated listening to music you couldn't have cared less about, reading dots on a piece of paper, and persistent pressure to practise for your next grade sound familiar? If so, you weren't alone.

And that's why the next chapter is all about how that happens, what causes it to persist, and why it's a problem for our children today.

WHAT WE GREW UP WITH ISN'T WORKING ANYMORE

'I'm Not Musical.'

I hear it all the time. After a parent sees their child performing at a concert, they'll say something like, 'That was great. I don't know where he/she gets it from though, as none of the family is musical.'

Sometimes it's about somebody who is musical: 'My grandmother/auntie/sister can just sit down at a piano and play so many songs. She picks it up by ear, it's amazing.'

After one parent told me she wasn't musical, I asked her how she knew that. She then said her flute teacher at school had told her off for not playing the right note and had said she wasn't cut out for music, before looking into the distance and sighing, 'It wasn't for me'. Another parent who was an accomplished musician herself told me that she knew her son wasn't musical, despite the fact he was playing in a band.

So what's going on here? What is 'being musical'?

It would seem to me that anyone who is playing music is being musical in some sense, and I know from experience that it's accessible to just about anybody on some level. Within five minutes, I can teach the large majority of people, whatever their age, to play a basic drum beat, a few notes on a guitar, or hit the right keys to take part in playing a song with others. In my eyes, that's the point of it: that's people being musical.

Yet when I've probed a bit deeper on the subject, there seems to be a belief that music is something you either have or you don't. I hear people saying things like 'I always wished I could play guitar' like it's a skill that would have been bestowed upon them if they were destined to be a musician. I also hear people who have learned to play an instrument quite successfully talk of others who can 'play by ear' as if it's a gift that very few are lucky enough to possess.

What all of this assumes is that being musical, the ability to play music, is something *fixed* – and you either have it or you don't. This is far from being true, but it is engrained in our culture surrounding music and the way we think of ourselves.

Think about it: if music was something only available to a gifted few, it would sit in a class of its own as a form of art and communication. It would mean that, unlike learning to speak, read, write, draw, etc., it isn't possible to learn the basic skills you need to partake.

How did you learn to draw, read and write? Were you perfect right away? Did people around you encourage you to give up and tell you that it wasn't your thing? Or did they persist with you, believing that you'd get there with enough practice?

Think about the journey your child is going on learning to do the same.

It's true that some people will be more naturally inclined towards some of these skills than others: they pick them up quickly, develop faster and show flair for the subject from the outset. But even if we allow for that, it would seem that most people consider music a much harder set of skills to acquire. So much so that you need to show talent and flair for it to even get going.

Why is this? How has the idea of music being a fixed ability become so engrained in our culture that it pops up so often when we talk about music lessons?

While there are probably many elements involved (and I'll save discussions on *X-Factor* and *Britain's Got Talent* for another time), I believe a large part of the answer lies in music being taught in its traditional format. Reading dots, practising scales, and learning theory and the like *is* really hard for most people and *does* require a substantial amount of mental processing to get started.

Learning to interpret sound through written music requires more than a few impressive mental tricks. To then process it fast enough to keep up on your instrument and co-ordinate your hands to play the right notes at the right time is an incredible feat of brain power, with many different functions firing at the same time.

In some ways, this is actually a good thing. Many studies have noted the power of learning an instrument for improving brain performance. But it does have its downsides too, especially if you're young and mental gymnastics isn't how you express your intelligence. To learn more about how this works, let's look at a typical first lesson through the eyes of child.

Symbols, Mathematical Concepts, Grid Systems And Ed Sheeran

Emily is six years old and has just seen Ed Sheeran on YouTube. She's not quite sure why, but his music video is one of the coolest things she's ever seen. It makes her feel good. She wants to be a part of it.

'Ed's really cool. I can do that. I want to do that,' she tells her parents. Being the supportive types and wanting the best for Emily, they enrol her in guitar lessons at school. It's her birthday in a month, and she doesn't know it yet, but she's got an instrument hiding in Mum and Dad's cupboard.

She turns up at her first lesson with gleaming eyes full of anticipation. This is going to be awesome.

When she arrives, there are music stands set out with pieces of paper on them. A friendly face says, 'Hi, I'm Mr Jones. We're going to learn the guitar.' Emily's still excited, but she doesn't think it quite looks like the sort of environment Ed Sheeran was playing in on the YouTube video.

Never mind, she thinks, *let's get cracking. I'm going to sound awesome.*

It can often be somewhere around this point that written music is introduced.

'See these five lines here? Those are called the stave.'

Now Emily has been in education for a while and is considered bright and conscientious. She likes to get things right and has a good track record of doing so. She can see that there are five lines just by looking.

Her classmate, George, an excitable child who took up guitar because he says yes to everything, is counting them. 'One, two, three... ' By the time he's got halfway, he's forgotten what they were called.

Emily says the word 'Stave' to herself to remember.

'This symbol at the start is called a treble clef, but let's not worry about that just now.'

A sensible choice made by the teacher, but it won't help Emily much, considering what is coming next.

'The numbers at the start say 4/4. This means we're going to count to four over and over again.'

At this point Emily's brain is starting to race. *Okay, so five lines and that was called something. Was it a treble something? And we've got to count to four. Why are there five lines then? Why are there two fours there?*

'This black note here is called a crotchet. That means it lasts one beat.'

Emily's brain goes into overdrive. Which of these things is most important? George is looking out of the window.

'And there are four of them in a bar... which we can tell by this line called a bar line.'

I thought there were five lines. What's this other line? It goes downwards. Don't all the black dots have lines?

'Now, this note between the third and the fourth of the five lines is called C.'

C, that's from the alphabet. The big alphabet. We've learned that one in class.

'When you see that you're going to press on this fret here with your first finger, left hand. It's the first fret on the second string.'

At this point, Emily's brain fries. George has long since switched off. The teacher has just introduced a grid system, totally alien to Emily as she hasn't learned about them at school, and won't for another two years. But Mr Jones presses on...

'Then with your right hand, you're going to pluck the string.'

Co-ordination and timing between two hands, not easy...

'And you're going to play it four times because there's four of them in the bar.'

Yes, I remember four!

'Okay, let's go.'

Let's now take stock of the mental gymnastics involved before our budding guitarists have even played their first note :

Five different numbers, two of which are in abstract form, two of which are relational through a grid system on the guitar and one of which relates to bodily awareness.

Two spatial awareness and shape recognition processes – where C is and the treble clef. One is relevant right now, one is distracting.

A letter that has been assigned a relationship to a number in a grid system and a shape. That looks something like shape/space – letter – grid reference.

Does it tie you in knots just reading that? What does it feel like? Complicated? Confusing? Annoying? That's how many children feel in early music lessons. George's response of shutting down was a perfectly sensible one. His processing power is not yet at a place where he can perform that task. Emily, being more concerned with getting things right, is in a highly stressful situation.

To add insult to injury, four Cs played on their own in isolation sound nothing like music. It's not the sort of thing Ed Sheeran was doing.

So, what are Emily's first impressions of music at this stage?

This is really, really hard. Am I any good at it? Maybe I can't do it.

What Mr Jones does next is absolutely crucial. Does he praise their efforts or notice whether it was right or wrong? It can make the difference between Emily persevering or giving up all hope.

Let's assume the teacher does well at this point. He praises Emily and George for their efforts and makes them feel good about what they've attempted to do. Emily breathes a sigh of relief and starts focusing on unravelling what happened. George smiles briefly and then goes back to staring out the window.

Mr Jones takes a deep breath. He understands that they're just getting started on a difficult mission. His job is to help Emily and George understand what they've got in front of them, and then in future weeks progress to more challenging material.

George has already lost interest and is thinking about building a spaceship. He will likely not continue past six months and will potentially start disrupting lessons. Emily will try hard to make Mr Jones happy, but it's no longer about the music. By the time George gives up she'll be able to play around six notes and read only the most basic rhythms. It's draining for her and draining for Mr Jones, but they'll battle on for a while.

So how do Emily and George end up thinking of themselves? As musicians? The chances are slim.

Battling Complexity

What most children do in the early stages is learn through watching what the teacher does and then copying it. Look closely – where is that finger? How many times are they playing that note? How does it sound? Over time the children get a feel for how it works, and eventually the connection to the written music starts to emerge.

Emily and George are learning music in school, which is where many children start. But it's not an environment where this method works very well. Depending on Emily's parents' level of engagement and resources, they have two routes to choose from in battling the inherent complexity of learning to read music:

1. Private lessons, intense focus and regular practice

2. Taking a long time to do it.

Option 1 is expensive and requires a lot of effort on the part of the child, teacher and parents, but it works.

Option 2 is a slog, but can also prove successful given enough years. Still, it requires a few cunning tricks to keep the momentum going.

Let's take a look at how it works:

Practice

Week after week, Mr Jones turns up to teach the children, and 90% of them have forgotten what they did last week. We're ten weeks in now, and while Emily is getting fairly fluent in the art of playing C, D and B, George is relentless in not remembering anything.

Mr Jones has been insisting to Emily and George, using his well-rehearsed stern voice at the end of lessons, that they practise. He's been sending home a practice diary for the parents to fill out. Emily's has been returned sporadically, but it's hard for her parents to keep on top of yet another piece of paperwork. George's has stayed in the bottom of his bag all term. When Mr Jones bumps into Emily's parents at the school gates, he tells them about how well she's doing, with an added reminder that ten minutes' practice a day is key.

Under these conditions, he's right to push for the children to practise at home. It's the only thing that will work. Performing such mental gymnastics requires regular repetition and focus. Once per week is not going to cut it in developing that sort of processing power. That's why Emily and George go to school and practise maths every day. They simply have to if they're ever to become competent at it.

The problem is, learning an instrument is extra-curricular. It's entered into voluntarily by Emily, George and their parents. Right now, it's hard, unnatural, boring and has nothing to do with Ed Sheeran. The chances of them *willingly* putting in the hours per week they're being asked to is close to nil. George doesn't even think about guitar between lessons. Emily's parents, being conscientious, have tried to help by insisting on ten minutes' practice every day before school. But it's hard to enforce when they're also busy and they know she's not enjoying it.

Exams

Could this be why exams were invented? I'm not sure, but it certainly seems to be how they're used as motivation in many cases. Enforcing practice is draining, but an exam on the horizon acts as both a carrot and a stick at the same time.

'If you do this practice and work really hard, you can take your Grade 1 exam and get a certificate!'

'If you don't practise, when the examiner asks you to play an F major scale, you're going to feel really bad if you don't know it. Then you might fail.'

Perhaps the F major scale particularly resonates with me because of an experience in my childhood. Like our heroes in Leopard Clone Wars and Lightning Beasts, I also played at the Portsmouth Guildhall as a child. But it was a bit different. I was doing my Grade 3 exam on the violin in one of the conference rooms. Instead of playing to 2,000 people, there were two other people in the room – my accompanist on the piano and an examiner.

I was easily as nervous as Lucas and Jack, if not more so. I was going to be marked... judged on how good I was. I would pass or fail.

The examiner studied me through narrow rimmed spectacles, scribbling furiously as I played. She greeted the end of the musical studies I'd learned with a stony silence. After what seemed like forever, she delivered the next instruction:

'Play me an F major scale, please.'

The exam up until the F major scale had been going quite well as I'd learned the pieces off by heart. They were musical, and therefore made sense. But remembering the F major scale – well, that was hard. It didn't seem to mean anything.

Two years earlier I had scored 106 on my Grade 1; last year with Grade 2 it was 103; now here I was in the middle of Grade 3 and feeling physically sick. I needed to score a total of 100 to pass the exam. If I got ninety-nine, I failed, which was a very real risk right now.

I scored 100.

I remember getting the results in the post. After feeling a temporary relief at having not failed (there's the stick in action), I looked ahead to what was next and felt a sinking feeling in my stomach.

Why on earth would I want to take Grade 4?

As it turned out I didn't have to worry about that. I got to secondary school and my new teacher quickly assessed that I 'wasn't good enough' to be working towards Grade 4 and should learn with the Grade 3 group. Great. This wasn't fun anymore. Any passion I had left for playing the violin died a death that day.

And many children follow a similar route. George never gets as far as exams, but Emily slogs it out. Now on exam day she gets to be judged. She'll do well, because she's Emily. When she receives her certificate and Mr Jones's praise, she'll experience a shot of feel-good chemicals that come from being told you can do something well. It's like the musical equivalent of being rewarded with a sweet. Because of this, Emily may get to Grade 2, or 3, or even surpass my meagre attempts and go further.

But then what?

It's All In The Name Of...Hang On, Why Are We Doing This?

Let's take stock of some of the things Emily and George have been learning through this process:

- Music is really hard

- It requires me to do something I don't want to, constantly

- If I keep doing this I'll gain the satisfaction of being judged favourably and a certificate

Along the way, there are many opportunities for them to conclude:

- I'm not musical, or I'm no good at the guitar

- Working hard at something is boring

- My self-worth is tied to a score that someone else determines

But what about the positives? Practice and exams in some circles are seen as virtuous ways to teach a child discipline. If the discipline develops from an external source (parents, teachers and exams) rather than from within (the child's motivation), then quite frankly, I don't think it's worth developing. It's fine while your child is getting results, but what's going to happen when you remove that external source of motivation? You'll probably find your child has become dependent on it and gives up easily. Not the answer most parents are looking for.

And where does it end? For George, it ended after around six months and he took home the belief that he's not musical. For Emily, she continued until she was twelve then figured that playing an instrument is stressful. As an adult, she'll be able to pick up a guitar and play a few tunes, but she's given up actively learning new things. She was never taught how to do that for herself. When her children ask her to play something, she'll say can't remember much and needs the music to play anything.

George will tell his children that he tried to play guitar but didn't take to it. He'll watch other people jam on instruments and say, 'I wish I could do that.'

Both of them have taken a hit to their confidence.

So why are we doing this? Is this what learning an instrument is supposed to be about? I've taught thousands of children over the years and I've put a total of two of them in for exams. In both cases, it was because the student wanted to do it, and I supported them in their choices. I always ask my students whether exams interest them, but most just shrug and say that's not why they want to play.

And that, at its essence, is what music is all about – playing.

I've had the good fortune to speak to countless people about what music means to them over the years, and they've told me it makes them feel amazing, it reminds them of good times or it moves them in some way. They've told me they enjoy playing it, listening to it and dancing to it.

Exams, practice and becoming highly skilled at a form of symbol interpretation called written music haven't showed up once. And that's why I set out to make a change.

3

TIME TO MAKE A CHANGE

The Roots

As a child, I vividly remember sitting down one weekend with my dad and watching a rerun of the Freddie Mercury benefit concert. There were so many different musicians playing songs that we all knew and loved by Queen, and it was very exciting to see how those different musicians interpreted them.

But my imagination was really captured during Elton John's rendition of 'Bohemian Rhapsody'. Just after the operatic build-up, with all of the 'Let Me Go's, fireworks marked the start of the head-banging rock section. A wild man with long ginger hair came careering onto the stage with an energy I'd never seen before. The crowd at Wembley Stadium were bouncing up and down and this man was spinning round, screaming into the microphone and commanding them with such spirit and charisma. It was like he'd taken all of his emotion, bottled it up and laid it bare on the stage in about two minutes. (Thanks to the wonders of the internet I've just watched it for the first time since on YouTube, and it still gives me shivers.) At the time, I remember thinking that was the coolest thing I'd ever seen.

'Who's that?' I asked.

'Guns N' Roses. That's Axl Rose, the lead singer.'

I knew I wanted to be a part of what was going on at Wembley. At some point in my life, I was going to have to be in a band. After watching everything on Guns N' Roses I could find on the music channels, I decided that guitar was going to be my thing.

I think Guns N' Roses were probably every parent's worst nightmare at the time, but my parents wanted to support me, so they bought me a child-size acoustic guitar from Argos and left me to my own devices. Within a few months I was going through my dad's tape collection and learning how to play lots of different songs on this exciting instrument. I was hooked.

This all happened during the last term of junior school while I was taking my Grade 3 violin. I asked the head of music at school about setting up a Year 6 band, but was told that the orchestra was my only option. I didn't mind too much though, as I was going to secondary school soon, and was enormously excited to learn that they had something called the Heavy Rock Club.

When I arrived at secondary school and found out the Heavy Rock Club was for geology enthusiasts rather than musicians, I had to take matters into my own hands. I decided to start a band, and went about persuading my friends to take up various instruments.

I was, and still am, extremely lucky to have had my dad's support throughout all this. Not only was he there at every rehearsal offering us words of encouragement, but he also took me to a local jam session every Monday night where I got to play with more experienced adult musicians. This was really a game changer, and within six months of first picking up a guitar I was a far more accomplished musician than I was after four years of violin lessons. Learning an F major scale was no problem at all when it contained the notes I needed to play a guitar solo over November Rain!

Over the course of secondary school, it was music that taught me many of life's lessons. From selling our act to a local venue to dealing with band members leaving, recruiting more people to join, disagreeing on which songs to play, building a following, learning how to work as a team, I was picking up valuable experience that has set me in good stead for other areas of life. But more than that, I felt like I was finally expressing who I was and who I had the potential to be. I enjoyed this, and I was keen to share it with anyone who would listen.

And On To Teaching

Perhaps it was because I'd experienced this more informal style of learning and had so much fun with it that I had no desire to impose anything on my students when I started teaching. I taught my first guitar lesson aged fourteen to an eight-year-old family friend, and I still remember our initial conversation quite vividly.

'So, what do you want to be able to do on the guitar?'

'I don't know.'

'Well, would you like to play a song by someone else or write your own song?'

'Write my own song!'

'Okay, cool. I'll play some chords and you tell me which ones you like.'

I strummed through some easy chords for a few minutes until he'd settled on two that he liked and then we got started. He's now twenty-five and a very capable guitarist all round.

My second student was a younger cousin of mine called David. We had the same conversation.

'So what do you want to do?'

This time the answer came back quick as a flash.

'Play Nirvana songs and play in a band.'

So we learned 'Smells Like Teen Spirit'. He played bass, I played guitar and we recorded it on a tape player. (Remember those?)

It wasn't long before David's friends showed up for lessons, and then friends of friends. I'd start with the same question every time: 'What do you want to do?' and we'd go from there. My job was nothing more than helping them to get to wherever they wanted to go, and in terms of results it was very successful. The large majority of my students from that period still play – most of them in bands or at home as a hobby, and a couple professionally. They all developed a passion for playing their instrument, not through me cracking the whip or using carrots and sticks, but through their own motivation.

I also had a brief spell of teaching in a few primary schools around this time, and was reprimanded early on for not teaching the children to read music. After asking what they wanted to play, I had started teaching them songs they had heard on the radio, not paying mind to the fact that they had spent the best part of a year working through a music reading book. While this went down well with the children, it seemed to baffle the parents and music service I was working for, so I dutifully went back to teaching the mental gymnastics routine.

Rocksteady Music School

After finishing university, I decided it was time to try and influence the way music was taught on a wider scale and set up a teaching business called Rocksteady Music School. I had the idea that it should be possible to transfer the success I'd had with private students to a mass audience, so I set about figuring out what that meant and how to go about it.

I gathered a few friends and ex pupils and we started teaching in community centres after school. We ran individual lessons and band workshops, focusing on what the people who came to us wanted to learn. There were younger children, teenagers and adults alike. I found myself teaching blues to a retired gentleman one lesson and a Kaiser Chiefs song to a seven-year-old the next.

One thing I noticed was that there were a few teenagers coming to us for lessons who had been playing for years but didn't seem to have the sort of musical awareness or ability

I would expect. They'd often had negative experiences with music as younger children, and there was a common belief that they 'weren't good'. In some instances we spent a lot of time undoing bad habits and working with poor self-confidence, which caused a fair amount of disruption in the lessons. At that point I began to see a need to make sure younger children's first experiences with music were positive ones.

Then something really interesting happened.

I got a phone call from a mother called Wendy whose son Seb had shown a keen interest in playing the electric guitar. He had just got one for Christmas, and was now a few days from his fifth birthday.

'Of course we can teach him,' I said. 'And of course we can teach his three friends who want to come too.'

I remember the first lesson vividly to this day, partly because nothing was working, and partly because Wendy was there to watch the whole thing!

Seb's ambition was to play rock music. We tried basic riffs of a few notes, but it was still a few notes too many. Putting your finger on the third fret (the metal bars on the guitar's neck) is a challenging concept when you've only just learned to count that far.

We tried strumming simple chords, but Seb's fingers weren't strong enough to hold them for more than a few seconds. We tried drawing pictures as a break from the intense physical activity of playing guitar, but drawing anything that could help with music was tough.

Watching Seb become discouraged as he tried time and time again but got nowhere was disheartening.

Eventually, against all my best intentions, we fell back on learning to read music for the time being. The exercises we were going through didn't sound anything like music, but at least we could tick them off and gain some sense of accomplishment.

Is this why so many younger children are taught this way? I wondered. The council's music service and other music schools at the time wouldn't even take five-year-olds for guitar lessons. It was recorder or nothing. I began to wonder if maybe there was a good reason for it.

But going back to my principles, I couldn't accept that teaching a young child the music that actually inspired him was proving less effective than teaching him to read music. I concluded that I simply hadn't learned enough and needed to get better at this, so I decided to offer our services where I could find the most young children, and picked up the phone to local primary schools.

A few of them were kind enough to work with me.

The Same Problem Multiplied

Once I started teaching in schools, I promptly became one of those 'bad' guitar teachers. If Seb struggled to get to grips with my teaching methods one on one, putting four highly energised children into a room together multiplied the problem. I was teaching children with different learning needs at the same time, and that made for very slow progress. If they were aged five or six, it was near impossible.

I reluctantly fell back on reading music (again!) and using the feeling of progressing to the next exercise to keep everyone motivated.

Behaviour problems arose as I tried to convince a disinterested group of seven-year-olds to play exercise five on page two for the fourth week running. I started issuing practice diaries that I hastily scribbled in and asked the children's parents to sign them. I found myself on the phone to parents explaining that if their children didn't practise, they wouldn't get anywhere.

Me, on the phone to parents, saying those things?

I realised this was not what I wanted to be doing for the children, but I could now fully understand why these methods of teaching had developed. They seemed like the only way to get any results for my pupils in this environment.

I spent the best part of a year in this mode, and watched some children give up and others stick it out painfully. It reminded me of my time learning the violin at school, where at least ten of us had started in Year 2, but there were only three left by the time we were in Year 6. Except this time I was on the other side of the fence. Why was there even a fence? Shouldn't we be on the same side?

My heart sank.

Fortunately I was about to discover another way.

Northern Parade

I got a phone call one day from a school who had read the standard letter I was sending out and thought that I was offering classroom music lessons rather than instrumental tuition. Would I like to interview to be their classroom music teacher for the whole school and teach 250 children in groups of thirty every week?

'Of course,' I said. 'I'll also run some lunchtime clubs and really get music kicking off at your school.'

I'm still not sure how I got through the interview and classroom observation, but later that evening I found myself accepting the job and getting prepared to teach four days per week at Northern Parade Junior School. I ended up staying there for three of the most enlightening years of my career.

It was a steep learning to curve to start with, as I was teaching every child in the school, including those who didn't care for learning anything about music. I soon discovered the best ways to engage children from all sorts of backgrounds, what made them tick and, just as importantly, what didn't.

During my lunchtime music clubs, I ran a school band. I had run band workshops before, but I'd never tried to teach eight children from scratch how to play their instruments, and play them in time together. We settled on a drummer, three guitarists, two keyboard players and two singers. I had no idea whether it would work or not, and most of the children didn't have instruments at home either, so I couldn't rely on asking them to practise. But the school was supportive of the experiment and the children were eager, so we gave it a go for half an hour, once a week at lunchtimes.

We set to work. Our first objective with the Year 5 band was to learn the White Stripes song 'Seven Nation Army' and play it at the Christmas concert. The drum part for this song is simple to grasp and we had figured out a keyboard part that would work, but I'd made the mistake of trying to keep the guitar parts the same as the original song. Concert time came round and it still didn't sound much like 'Seven Nation Army', but we had committed ourselves to the challenge, and weren't going to back out.

'That Was Awesome!'

A mere ten weeks after they had started playing their instruments the Year 5 band found themselves on stage, with me announcing to the school that they were going to play 'Seven Nation Army' by the White Stripes. What they played was *something* like 'Seven Nation Army' in that it had some of the same notes in it, but they were mostly played at the wrong time and in the wrong order, and when you multiply that across the six people playing in the band, you end up with an interesting soup of sound that you probably wouldn't describe as music. Despite this, however, the concert was considered a resounding success.

As the school filtered out of the hall, the Executive Head, Sue, came over to greet me.

'Well, it's a start...' I offered as Luke, the guitarist from the band, came running over.

'That. Was. Awesome! I want to do it again!'

Sue smiled and gave me a knowing nod. And right there and then, in that hall in December, something clicked into place. I had seen many school Christmas concerts before, but this one was different. It actually hadn't mattered that the musicians weren't playing perfectly. For once that didn't seem to be the point. This was the children's first time on stage in front of other people playing these instruments and they had actually enjoyed the experience. There was no need to motivate them to want to do it again; motivation was already there in spades. As long as they were having fun, they were going to get something out of it.

Luckily for me, Sue was on exactly the same wavelength. 'I look forward to seeing the next one,' she said, and promptly booked the band to play at every event she could find in the school calendar.

When we came back to school after the Christmas break, the children arrived with a new found energy and enthusiasm. I would hear them in in the corridors talking about who was going to stand where on stage and whether there was room for a guitar solo in the next song. Did Luke even know how to play a guitar solo? What outfits were they going to wear? Would it be possible to have backing vocals?

In rehearsals they doubled their efforts and focused intently on the next concert. They quickly learned the basics of how to play in time with each other, listen to what was going on in the band and how songs were put together. By the time they had been playing a year, their skills on the individual instruments far surpassed anything I'd seen before at primary school level. There was something about playing with other people in a band and performing at concerts that made everything click into place.

Harry

The final piece of the puzzle slotted into place when I met Harry. I'd noticed Harry in classroom music lessons when he was in Year 4. He was, and probably still is, a bright boy who enjoyed music, but he had low self-esteem and a lot of trouble accepting positive recognition for his efforts. This led to some form of disruptive behaviour in most lessons and he would frequently escalate any situation into a confrontation.

I was setting up a second school band and wanted him to be involved. For our first band meeting, I found a few children who had expressed an interest in being a part of it, and asked them to go and find Harry.

Five minutes later, he came storming into the room.

'What have I done wrong?' he asked, ready for a fight.

'Hi, Harry, thanks for coming. Take a seat.'

'No. Not until you tell me what I've done.'

'We just wondered if you wanted to be in the Year 5 band.'

'What, *me*?'

'Yep, you.'

He sat down, cautiously.

'What would you like to play?' I asked him.

'Ummm, drums, I think'.

'Well, we already have a drummer, but do you know about the bass guitar? That's the instrument that connects the drummer to the rest of the band.'

'No, what's that?'

Our journey began. At the time we only had a full-sized bass guitar, and learning an instrument that requires quite some strength to hold for half an hour per week is no mean feat for a nine-year-old. He found it tough and occasionally got frustrated with himself, but he persisted. He was determined to do this.

Within ten weeks Harry played his first school concert with his band. Within ten months he played the Portsmouth Guildhall. Not only did he play 'Forget You' by Cee Lo Green with his band, he also backed the inter school choir for two songs, playing 'Eye of the Tiger' and 'Harder, Better, Faster, Stronger' by Daft Punk. He came to the venue with me before the event, helped sound-check the equipment, and generally worked hard all day.

This marked quite a change in his attitude, not just towards others, but towards himself. He was doing something that he was good at and had been trusted to do.

I wasn't the only one who was impressed with what Harry and his band did that day. After the concert, a secondary school teacher approached me.

'How are you doing this? We've never seen children that young so capable before.'

The truth is, it wasn't so much me who was doing it as them. Yes, I had to show them where the notes were, help them out when they were finding things difficult and emphasise the importance of playing in time, but these things aren't nearly as difficult when the people you're teaching are motivated by themselves.

By the time Harry was in Year 6 he'd been selected by the teachers as a prefect and had moved to the top maths group. I remember listening to him confidently explain to an Ofsted inspector what playing in a band meant to him.

Learning to play an instrument and be part of a band had given him far more than just technical skill on the instrument. He'd developed the ability to listen to others and work as a team. And most important of all, he'd developed the confidence to say 'Yes, I can do that' when faced with a new situation.

Let's Take It To The World

If there was one Harry out there, there were a million. I strongly felt it was time to get what I'd learned into a method so that other musicians could deliver it and get it out to the world. Much like the teaching style, I didn't want our training system to be a rigid set of instructions. Instructions were the very things causing the problem.

I sat down with the other people at Rocksteady and came up with seven principles of teaching music Rocksteady style:

1. Make it fun

2. Inspire first and teach second

3. Play in a band and play concerts

4. Teach songs the children love

5. Teach music as a language

6. Make it as relevant and accessible as possible

7. Build the whole person.

I wish it had just been three – much easier to remember – but I felt then, and still feel today, that all seven are necessary.

The rest of the book is dedicated to exploring where the principles came from, how we use them and why they work for children of all backgrounds.

PART 2
PROGRESSION THROUGH SELF EXPRESSION

Chapter 4: Starting On The Right Note

Chapter 5: Musicians As Role Models

Chapter 6: Learn Music As A Language

We'll be doing some heavy lifting in this part of the book as we explore what's going on behind the Rocksteady model and what we believe is important in education.

In Chapter 4 we'll tap into the core motivation behind wanting to learn an instrument and why we believe it's vital not only to listen to children, but also let them lead their own learning.

In Chapter 5 we'll look at the power of positive role models in education. Who the teacher is matters just as much, if not more, than what they know.

In Chapter 6 we'll look at how reading music came to be the standard for learning how to play an instrument and why it doesn't make nearly as much sense today.

STARTING ON THE RIGHT NOTE

Jennifer has to work hard at getting her child Riley to practise the clarinet. When Jennifer was a child, she wasn't allowed to eat breakfast before she'd practised her piano. It worked: she learned to play well. But it's different with Riley. Perhaps he puts up a bit more resistance; perhaps there are hundreds of TV channels, computer games and an iPad that are calling for his attention. Perhaps he senses that playing the clarinet isn't relevant to the rest of his life.

Either way, practising before breakfast is a tough routine to keep enforcing. It's a drain for Riley, but also for Jennifer. She wants to make sure that Riley learns *and* enjoys the clarinet at the same time.

When an opportunity for Rocksteady lessons came up at school, Riley was desperate to play the drums. Wanting to support Riley in his enthusiasm, Jennifer signed him up. He started a year ago and has been mad about it ever since. He goes to band practices, learns rock and pop music and performs in front of the school. Jennifer recently bought him a drum kit and he wants to play on it non-stop, to the point she's had to put restrictions around it to keep peace with the neighbours. Slowly but surely, Riley's improving at both the drums and, oddly enough, the clarinet too.

So what's going on here? Why is Riley so much more keen to play the drums than practise his clarinet?

It's all about his own motivation. The incentive for practising the clarinet comes from external things, such as his teacher or his mum. The incentive for playing the drums comes from within.

Why Do Children Want To Learn Instruments?

We've touched on why children might want to learn music more than a few times already. It's the central theme running through this book, and for good reason. There's a lot of focus in education on what children are doing and how they should be doing it, but why they should be doing it is often missing.

Motivation for most people, children included, lives in this 'why' space rather than the 'what' or the 'how', so it's an important part to get right. As parents and teachers, we want children to grow up to be happy, confident and independent. And unless we can tap into their own internal motivation and teach them to use it, we'll likely fall down on all three counts.

Back when I first started Rocksteady, I felt it was important to understand why children want to pick up instruments in the first place, so I spent a few weeks having conversations with my students and recording my findings. A bit further down the road, I did a survey. The results broke down into the following categories:

- Because I want to be cool and impress my friend and family – 90%

- Because I love the sound of my instrument or my favourite band and want to do the same – 10%

How interesting. While it may be moments like the Ed Sheeran one for Emily that provide the spark of inspiration for children to get going, lying behind this is a desire to be someone, and to show this someone to other people. As adults we might feel slightly uncomfortable to imagine our reasons for taking up this wonderful art are rooted in vanity, but children have less problems with such honesty.

If we look at more general models of how humans are motivated, it makes a lot of sense.

Maslow's Hierarchy Of Needs

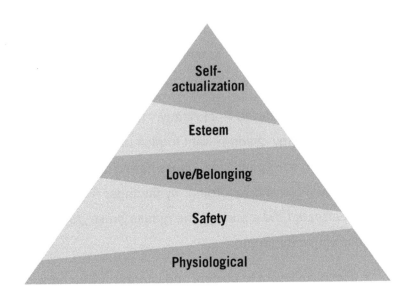

This model is known as Maslow's hierarchy of needs. Famed psychologist Maslow used this in his 1943 paper 'A Theory Of Human Motivation' to describe the stages motivation moves through. It's represented as a pyramid because our most basic needs are at the bottom, leading to the more advanced ones at the top. Once we've got a stage covered, we look to the next one.

Physiological needs are the basics for our survival, such as food, adequate warmth, clothing and shelter. The theory states that once we've secured these, we look towards safety for ourselves and loved ones – security and freedom from various types of harm.

The love and belonging stage is interesting, because while it comes above physiological and safety needs in the pyramid, it can take centre stage over them at various points in life, especially in children. This stage is about the need to feel you belong and are accepted among your social group, whether that's your family, your workplace or your class at school.

The esteem stage is all about confidence, and we find this through feeling that we are valued, making a contribution and building self-respect. This stage is slightly more complex and in some ways quite delicate. Maslow noted two different forms of esteem, one that was achieved through a need for status, recognition and attention, and another that came through building competence, self-confidence and independence.

Self-actualisation is about fulfilling our full potential in life, whether that's painting our masterpiece, winning the Olympics or becoming the best parent wecan be.

So what does all this have to do with learning to play an instrument? Well, if your child comes from a stable and supportive family, it's likely that their physiological and safety needs are already being met. A good proportion of their love and belonging needs will also be met at home, so the next stages are building their capabilities for securing love and belonging across a wider variety of peer groups and putting in place the foundations for esteem.

This is where the desire to learn new skills and be recognised for them comes from. Learning an instrument that's considered 'cool' by your peer group and showing people what you can do with it is a very healthy way of expressing these needs.

Different Shades Of Cool

When I dug a little deeper with the children, I realised there were a lot of subtleties regarding what our 90% meant by being cool and impressing their friends and family. Some children meant 'making people happy'. Some meant 'creating excitement'. Some meant 'creating an identity for myself'. Some meant 'I want to gain approval'.

It all depends on where your child is on their journey and what their specific strategies for gaining love, belonging and esteem are.

There are different shades of being cool, different shades of impressing, and it's a deeply personal thing, even to a five-year-old. Try quizzing your child about this and listening carefully to what they say. It can be quite a fascinating conversation.

What was clear with every single child I asked, however, was that it was important to them when learning an instrument to have the opportunity to share this achievement they were so proud of. Unlike solving a Rubik's cube, meditating or doing a jigsaw puzzle, musicians are motivated to play for other people. They want to create some sort of emotion for both their audience and themselves.

So, with being cool and impressive as the driving force behind learning, let's take a closer look at how this manifests itself, and what our budding musicians want to learn along the way.

They Want To Play Concerts – The Bigger, The Better

They want to play concerts that feel like 'real life' concerts, by which they mean they want it to be as close to what they've seen on YouTube or TV as possible. Ask your child what's impressed them about other musicians and you'll get a good idea of what their aspirations are. It makes good sense if you want to learn how to play music – what could be more cool and impressive than showing the world on a big stage?

A good example of a child who's gained a lot from performing is someone I used to teach at Northern Parade called Shanaya. Shanaya and her twin sister Kaleigh have been playing keyboard and singing in bands for the whole of their primary school career.

It all started on the day of the Christmas concert in Year 3 when, despite not belonging to a band at the time, Shanaya decided there was no reason why she shouldn't join in. The only problem was, it after school and none of the teachers or her parents had expected her to be doing it.

I watched in awe as she persuaded the choir leader that she would be perfectly able to sing with no rehearsals, and then spent the best part of half an hour after school convincing her dad to pick her up at 6pm, despite both parents being at work.

After Shanaya had got up on stage and sung, she was hooked. She returned in January, eager to learn the keyboard so that she could support her singing and became an integral part of the school's musical culture.

I spoke to Shanaya in July 2015, just after she'd played her last primary school concert. During the concert she took it upon herself to play parents in with an Adele song, then she performed an Ellie Goulding song with her band as the main event. Afterwards she stood up in front of the school and parents and thanked her music teachers for all they had done for her over the years.

She had come a long way from being the bundle of energy I used to teach in Year 3 and I wanted to find out about her journey. She recalled the twenty or so opportunities she'd had to perform, from summer festivals in the city to school celebrations. Each one meant something to her and had propelled her on to the next.

The more Shanaya played, the more she wanted to play. And the more she wanted to play, the better she got and the more confidence she built in her abilities.

I've experience this myself as a musician. After a gig, you've have so much fun that you start thinking about the next one. It gives you something to work towards and creates the focus needed to improve and build your confidence.

They Want To Play With Their Friends And Make New Friends

Part of belonging is doing things with other people and working towards something as part of a team. This can be a large team, such as a whole class, or a smaller team, such as a band or a sports team.

Music offers a great route into this world for many children. Their common goal is playing a concert for their fans. There's a more artistic slant to music than to many team activities, and the outcome they're striving for can be quite individual while still playing in a group.

The thing about music that appealed to me was that the rules were less fixed. We could be a rock band, a pop band, a metal band, or create some interesting and bizarre sounds that no one had ever heard before. It came with a lot of freedom and was a lot of fun.

They Want To Be Taught By A 'Real' Musician

Children are always searching for role models, which is an essential part of healthy development. In order to be a role model to children, you need to be someone they aspire to be.

In my early days teaching classroom music, many of the other teachers commented on how different my lessons seemed to be. The first thing I showed the children was how to put together their own performance of 'We Will Rock You'.

'Very different from the old teacher' was the classroom assistant's assessment.

I found myself wondering if different was a good thing, but the children soon chimed in and put my mind at ease.

'This is so much better than when we had Mrs Brown.'

'Why's that?' I asked, curious as to what was going so right. The answer I got back was surprisingly similar each time.

'It's more fun because you can play all these things and know about lots of songs.'

'I'm sure Mrs Brown could play different instruments and knew a lot of songs.'

'Yeah, but only because she was a music teacher. You're in a real band and play real concerts.'

The fact that I was teaching them seemed incidental. What was important to the children was that I lived and breathed what they wanted to be able to do. They didn't seem to identify me as a music teacher as much as a musician.

When I started hiring and training different people to teach, I observed the same thing time and time again. Those who were most successful were musicians first, and teaching was just another way of sharing this awesome part of life with others.

They Want To Play Cool Songs

Despite always priding myself on teaching exciting songs, I remember one particular lesson in 2012 where we were exploring lyrics. Just to see how far we could take it, I played the children an Arctic Monkeys' song, thinking I was playing something perfectly modern and attractive to people of the time.

A child put their hand up.

'Who is this and why do we have to listen to old music?'

Ouch. My aim at sharing lyrical genius from the Arctic Monkeys had missed the mark.

'Okay,' I replied, 'what would you like to listen to?'

'Call Me Maybe' by Carly Rae Jepsen came up, as did 'Paradise' by Coldplay and the ever present One Direction. Paradoxically, Michael Jackson and Journey were also on the list. Some of the music was new and some was a lot older than the Arctic Monkeys' song, but old or new didn't seem to be the point. The point was to find a song the children perceived as 'cool'. Would they want to play it to their friends?

From then on, I worked very hard at getting inside the minds of these young musicians. I listened intently to what they were talking about and did my homework. Part of building their belonging and esteem involves playing songs they can relate to and be proud of, and whether we like it or not, these can be very different to the songs we identify with – no matter how 'cool' we are!

They Want To Have Fun

In order to learn an instrument, play in a band and deal with the nerves of concerts, children have to work incredibly hard. And having fun is the glue that holds everything together when things get tough. Fun is not being silly or acting up: the dictionary definition of fun is 'informal', and I think this describes what the children are talking about quite accurately.

When you're self-motivated, a culture of formality and strictness is often a hindrance rather than a help. With learning in general, and especially in an artistic endeavour like music, too much structure and formality can get in the way of what you're trying to do.

Shanaya summed it up perfectly after her last concert.

'I'm happy that you guys are teaching people these things because I like the way that I'm having fun while I'm playing music, and I love to play music because I'm having fun. It's the same thing.'

I couldn't have said it better myself.

Pushing And Pulling In Education. Why I Believe In Pulling

This chapter has been all about why children want to play and what they want from their lessons. You might very reasonably ask, 'Should we be giving children what they want? Are they really best placed to know what's good for them?' After all, as adults we have the benefit of experience. We've been through their stage of life and feel we know what's going to be best for them.

It's an interesting question, and is a philosophical point as much as anything. When I first realised what drives children to learn music, I had a choice about what to do with that information. I could have decided that they 'needed' to learn to read music in order to be a musician, and if they couldn't cut it, well then it wasn't for them. I could have decided that learning scales was in their best interests and they would thank me for it further down the road... if they ever got there. I could have decided that they needed to learn traditional music, rock music, or whatever I felt was most important to gain a good basis. I could have banned any *X-Factor* related material from my lessons – a very tempting one for me!

We're always faced with making judgments on what we should or shouldn't be promoting to the next generation and it's not an easy balance to strike. It can seem like the right thing to impose our views on what children should be interested in, but this approach has a few serious drawbacks.

Firstly, it requires a lot of effort on the part of the adult as it's their drive rather than the child's that's producing the energy and motivation. Secondly, teaching in this manner creates a dependency on the teacher for that motivation, and what happens when they're not there? Every parent who's banged their head against the wall trying to get their child to practise at home knows the answer to that.

If instead of pushing what we believe about music on to children, we pull on their core motivations and enthusiasm for music, quite the opposite happens. We create commitment. And what happens then when the teacher's not around? Well, if we've done our job properly, the motivation is still there, and we've given our pupils the commitment and ability to learn by themselves. I'll take that over my beliefs on what music education 'should' be any day.

I believe the same goes for other areas of education, be it maths, English, art or sport. If a child got over the finish line because their teacher 'pushed' them, it may produce a short term result, but if it's at the expense of their independence and ability to learn new things in the long term, is it really worth it?

In my view, the long-term goal of any teacher should be to equip people with the tools to learn by themselves. This type of teaching requires a skilled person who can build awareness, responsibility and independence in their pupils. It is harder, takes longer and requires an enormous amount of commitment to the group or individuals being taught. And that's why the next section is all about musicians as role models.

MUSICIANS AS ROLE MODELS

It's my general observation that people want to learn from someone who is a living example of where they want to be. You see Jamie Oliver's meals and you want to know how he did that. Or you see a fitness programme written by the Olympic medallist Bradley Wiggins on Facebook and you want to know what his training involves. In my case it's seeing David Gilmour from Pink Floyd talking about guitar tones on the front of a magazine. You get the picture.

The reason budding chefs listen to Jamie Oliver is because he cares about cooking and is brilliant at it. They want to cook like him. The reason keen cyclists listen to Bradley Wiggins is because he's already been on the journey and become a champion and icon as a result. I'll listen to David Gilmour because I'd love to make my guitar sound as good as his. All three have the skills we desire. Add a healthy dose of passion to their ability, and we'll hang on every word.

Your child is no different. Their musical inspiration comes from musicians who can play well and impress others. And failing that, they're inspired by people who share the same enthusiasm for the particular parts of music they care about.

So given this insight, what is a music teacher's job exactly? When a school or parent pays a specialist to come in and teach children about music, what are they expecting for their money?

The obvious place to start is to look at the literal meaning of the job role, which is to teach children about music. The instrument teacher's role, whether they're a guitar teacher who visits weekly, an orchestra leader or even a Rocksteady band leader, is about imparting the skills needed to play the instrument. But if we dig a little bit deeper, building a child's capability on the instrument is only one part of the equation. There's a great opportunity to do so much more.

Musicians Or Music Teachers?

In the last chapter, I spoke about the difference between musicians and music teachers through the eyes of a child. Children are very perceptive about authenticity; they can tell if someone is the real deal or not, and they care about it much more than we might think.

A story that illustrates this comes from my early days experimenting at Northern Parade. I brought in some musicians I worked with to teach keyboard, drum and guitar lessons on the days of the week the band wasn't rehearsing. One day, while we were teaching a classroom lesson, the school had visitors pop in to see what we were doing, and one of our most avid young musicians had the job of showing them around.

'This is Rocksteady Music School. They come in and teach us, but really they're a band who play concerts all over the country,' he explained to the interested visitors. It struck me as slightly amusing, but it was the passion in the child's voice that really hit me. A big part of why he was hanging on every word we said was that we were musicians out there doing the things that inspired him, even if it was only at weekends. We weren't just teachers, we were also role models.

The traditional music teacher, by contrast, imparts a different feeling. Their focus is much more in line with their job title: less about inspiring and more about teaching than music. As such, it feels pre-planned to the child, and often it is. The music teacher has an agenda (often called a lesson plan) that's designed to impart something they know to the child, usually following a curriculum determined by somebody who's a long way from the people in the room. The child has no choice in the matter, and just knowing this is enough to bring out a rebellious streak in some.

If the music teacher is skilled, they will have planned their lesson around the needs of the children in the room, but there's still a disconnect between what the child and teacher want out of the lessons. The child wants to have fun, play with others, play concerts and learn from an inspirational musician. The traditional music teacher wants to teach the child a set of skills, and planning the lessons around the children's needs is simply a way to get there. To the child it can feel like something that's being done *to* them rather than *for* them, and it doesn't often bring about great results.

Wouldn't it be much better if the person teaching music was an inspirational musician who was motivated towards the same outcomes as the children? I certainly thought so.

The Other Parts Of The Job – Being A Role Model And What This Means Beyond Teaching Music

The main difference between the two approaches is that the musician, as well as teaching the child to play the instrument, has the opportunity to serve as a role model.

So what is a role model and why is it important? One dictionary defines a role model as:

A person looked to by others as an example to be imitated.

And when the dictionary says imitated, it's not just talking about imitating the tutor's limbs when playing a Pharrell song on the drums. It's also talking about imitating the values, choices and character of the role model.

Children are searching for such people all the time. They start at home with their parents, then look to their wider environment as they get older. The core of who they are, their values and motivations, is set early on in life, but their behaviour, skills and experience are constantly adapting and changing as life moves forward. They look to role models in order to learn about different skills and strategies, helping them manage new situations as they arise.

Every parent and teacher knows that, while you strive to be a great example for children, it is not a job that you do alone. Making sure children have a variety of positive people around them to look up to is part of healthy, rounded development. For many children, music is an exciting aspect of life, and the person teaching music has a great opportunity to step into a role model's shoes.

Children are also more receptive to learning from someone they consider to be a role model, which works well for both their behaviour in class and the speed at which they learn new skills. A person attempting to teach when they're not perceived as a role model has a difficult job. They often find themselves having to stand their ground with disinterested children. They are forced to create a culture of imposed discipline (different from self-discipline). Carrots and sticks become the currency.

A role model, on the other hand, has a fun and rewarding job and uses inspiration as their currency. They're often full of stories about their experiences with different bands and concerts they've played at the weekend. They share ideas with their pupils and get excited when the pupils bring ideas to them.

One has the opportunity only to impart a skill. The other has the opportunity to build skill, confidence and act as an example for children to model their behaviour on.

What Makes A Great Role Model? What You Know And Who You Are

We're picky about who we select to be band leaders at Rocksteady. Very picky, because we know it's the single most important decision we make in determining the success of your child's music lessons. If we select someone with great musical ability who can play every instrument under the sun, but they don't demonstrate passion towards learning, your child won't be passionate about learning themselves. If we hire someone who is passionate about what they're doing but doesn't have the right level of ability in dealing with children, their messages won't get through. If we find someone who is great at managing children but can't wow the kids from time to time with a cool guitar riff, the children won't consider them role models and will quickly disengage.

Finding the person who can fill these shoes isn't easy, but we've worked on it over a number of years and have got pretty good at spotting the special and uniquely talented people required. What's interesting about the three qualities is that each one comes from a different place. One is experience, one is taught and one is innate.

For our band leaders, musicianship is largely gained through a wealth of experience. They need to have years of playing in bands behind them and hundreds of stories up their sleeve. Ability with children is something that we train in house. It's a complex and ever evolving mix of skills, but it's based primarily around listening carefully to children in order to determine their mindset, how they're feeling and which learning styles will suit them. Once we've listened, then we need to have the appropriate communication skills.

What we can't teach, however, is passion. I know this from experience, having tried more than once. Whether it's a passion for the music itself or a passion for sharing it with the next generation, both need to be present in equal amounts to be successful in the job. What's more, the world needs to be able to see this passion for it to inspire, so our band leaders tend to be people who wear their hearts on their sleeves. They will happily strike up a conversation about music or teaching at the drop of a hat and keep you talking well into the night.

Inspire First, Teach Second

In Chapter 3, I listed one of our core beliefs as 'inspire first and teach second'. This is all about getting a child's mind ready to learn before we do the teaching. The best teachers at school are always the ones who give their class a compelling reason to want to learn, whatever the subject is. The children should have a full understanding of what the question is from a number of angles and be aching to know the answer.

At Rocksteady we take this seriously, and there's perhaps no better demonstration than our assembly and workshop days.

Our most recent full time inspirer, Matt Palmer, played at Rocksteady's first Battle Of The Bands as a student many years ago. Now, he visits a new school almost every day, and shares his enthusiasm for playing in a band with upwards of 40,000 children per year. He has more energy than any child you'll ever meet, can play a range of instruments, and his personality is almost as large as his hair. To top it off, he's the loudest person I've ever known. The perfect storm.

As the children walk in, he picks up his guitar and plays and sings to create the right atmosphere from the word go. At the time of writing, his repertoire includes songs by Bruno Mars, Ellie Goulding and Pharrell Williams – songs children can and do sing along to. He insists on it.

'When I was younger, it was all about being in my band and trying to become famous,' says Matt. 'Now I play in my band for fun, but still get to be a rock star every day to the kids I see.'

He's right. As the children walk into the hall, he is as close to a rock star as most of them have witnessed in the flesh.

He takes this responsibility very seriously. 'It's my job to entertain them, but also to inspire them. They could all become musicians if they wanted to be. It's my job to show them they can.'

And show them he does. After playing them all in, he greets them.

'This assembly is all about music!' he shouts. The windows rattle. 'It's about picking your favourite instrument, playing in bands and having fun.

'Music is exciting, and when you're excited it's okay to make a lot of noise, so we're going to practise doing just that. After the count of three, I want you to cheer as loud as you can. ONE, TWO, THREE... '

The children go wild, but he only needs to step forward and put his finger on his lips for silence to fall over the room. They're in the palm of his hands, not because he's enforced any sort of discipline, but because they really want to know what he's going to say next.

He shows them the electric guitar and how loud the amplifier can go. He shows them drums and drum solos, teaching the children to clap along during the beats and cheer when he plays fast drum fills. He plays Adele songs on the keyboard and demonstrates how to use a microphone properly if they want to be 'the most important person in the band'. All the while, he's encouraging them to think about which instrument they would like to play if they could.

'What part would you like to play in a band?'

By the time the workshops come along later in the day and the children have a go themselves, they're hanging on every word. They learn about the importance of listening and playing in time. They learn about playing the same notes as the other instruments and making sure they happen at exactly the right time. They learn the importance of singing like you mean it and the basics of stage presence. They have a great experience and take home lessons about playing an instrument they'll remember.

And they remember because Matt took the time to make sure they were inspired first.

This carries over to the weekly lessons too. All Rocksteady band leaders are great players in their own right, and the children know it.

One of the longest serving members of our team, Mike Heelan, often tells new recruits a story about when we first introduced a bass guitar to lessons. The bass guitar is the electric guitar's bigger and deeper sounding cousin, and many of the children hadn't seen it in action before.

'Who wants to be the bass guitarist?' he asked. No hands went up and a little bickering went on about who was going to be forfeiting the electric guitar to play one with four strings. So Mike picked up the bass and played a few flashy riffs on it. The children sat in awe.

'So is everyone sure they don't want to be the bassist?' This time the children were all so eager they had to agree to take turns over the coming weeks.

Isn't it nicer to have to take turns on something everyone wants to do rather than be forced to do something no one wants? The difference is all in that small but very effective dose of inspiration.

Listening – It's Not Just For Children

The whole Rocksteady method is founded upon listening. Let's revisit the seven principles we follow:

1. Make it fun

2. Inspire first and teach second

3. Play in a band and play concerts

4. Teach songs the children love

5. Teach music as a language

6. Make it as relevant and accessible as possible

7. Build the whole person.

Each one came from listening to children, parents and teachers and making constant adjustments until we got there. As adults, we often tell children to listen to us, and I've seen more than one occasion where an adult has said 'You're not listening!' to a child when they're not grasping something.

Jack B, our drummer from the Lightning Beasts in Chapter 1, is a quiet, thoughtful child. He generally doesn't put himself forward for things and shies away from situations where he has to participate with others. He doesn't like school, so much so that he's often quite anxious about going at all.

'He gives me trouble getting ready in the mornings,' explains Mum Emma, 'but never on a Wednesday, because that's Rocksteady day.'

She continues, 'Luke, his band leader, is very encouraging and lifts his spirits. He feels like he's good at something, and it's been a huge boost to his confidence.'

Luke sees it like this. 'Jack's mum Emma is one of the most supportive parents I know. She would do anything to help Jack progress on the drums, and I think this energy has come down to Jack, as he's always so supportive to the rest of the band. He's sort of the glue that keeps them together.'

What's interesting about this is that Luke knows not just what Jack can do, but *who* Jack is and what motivates him. Having an ability to hold people together and support each of their individual personalities is an enormously valuable skill set in life. Luke has recognised it as a core motivation for Jack and has encouraged it along with his drumming. As such, both Jack's drumming and his confidence have taken off.

Luke was able to do this because he listened carefully. Once he'd listened and knew what was important to Jack, he could help Jack grow and choose the right language, communication and praise to suit Jack's unique set of traits and skills. What's even more interesting is that Luke knows these things about all of his pupils. It's what makes him a great teacher.

A Different Kind Of Respect

At Rocksteady, we believe a great teacher is someone who models values and behaviour and then gives the children the space they need to grow. They don't impose their will on the children unless there's urgency in the situation, and they're open about mistakes they make in their own learning.

David is another child who struggles with school. Not academically – he's very bright in that respect – but he does struggle with wanting to be there in the first place. He doesn't want to go to any after school clubs or activities, even if he's interested in the subject matter they're covering (he sees them as more structure to endure), and transitioning between years has been a challenge. Moving into Year 1, he wasn't sure he wanted to go to school at all.

'But Rocksteady drew him in,' explains his mum, Dianne. 'He has such good fun. And it's through having fun that he's learning to listen to others, improving his spatial awareness, his confidence and his general interaction with music.'

What's interesting for Dianne to watch is that while David becomes very stressed during school plays and assemblies, he practically jumps out of bed for playing concerts with his band.

'When it's a school play, he's conscious of being in the spotlight. There's lots to remember, things that have to be done. He feels like he has to get it right for an external authority. With Rocksteady concerts, he feels a lot more in control. He gets to choose his own clothes, he's playing a song that he feels a part of, and it's much more expressive of who he is. They're given space.'

Space is an interesting topic and one that keeps coming up in our conversation.

'Richard, their band leader, allows them space to be themselves. It's impressive how he manages to lead the lessons so organically but is still very much on top of things when he needs to be. The children call him by his first name and have a playful relationship with him, but they very much know where the boundaries are. After the concert, they were jumping up and pulling on his beard, which is a totally different relationship to the one they usually have with their teachers. It's a different sort of respect.'

People can grow under pressure, or they can grow when you give them space to do so. Very much like the pushing and pulling examples we talked about in the last chapter, one is much harder to do, but the results are more than worth it. Part of creating space for children to grow is making it okay to try things, make mistakes and learn from the experience.

Luke talks about teaching the Lightning Beasts:

'I realised a little while ago that if I can make the lessons as safe as possible for the children, they won't mind making mistakes. Once this revelation lands, the bands usually go from strength to strength. They even ask for harder parts and go home and practise them!'

And there you have it: practice coming from a place of personal motivation, made even stronger by the teacher creating a truly supportive environment.

It's one thing to say, it's another thing entirely to achieve. One thing I've heard Luke say a few times in lessons is 'Sorry, my mistake.' How often do you hear that in adult/ child relationships? It takes bravery, but it produces great results. By giving himself the freedom to try new things, the permission to get it wrong sometimes and being honest about the situation with the children he's teaching, Luke's creating the space for himself to grow and actively modelling the behaviour for the children in his group. He's become a role model.

And that is just as valuable, if not more so, than being able to play something note perfect.

LEARN MUSIC AS A LANGUAGE

Emily and George, the children in Chapter 2, struggled with learning an instrument, and a large part of that was down to how they were being taught. They were learning to make decisions on what to play based on written music, much like a person who learns what to say based on reading the lines of a Shakespeare play.

There's nothing inherently wrong with learning to read music, and as we shall see, it's essential for certain musical pursuits. However, it's important to use the right tool for the right job and look at the context the children are learning in.

To understand a little bit more, let's look at why reading music used to be the best way to get started.

Reading Music Was Awesome...

Picture the scene. Its 1802 and you're eight years old. You live in a wealthy household. Your father's in business, your mother's time is dedicated to raising you, and you have a few hired hands helping out round the house.

You walk down the stairs to breakfast and you hear the opening movement of Beethoven's Piano Sonata No. 14 in C sharp minor coming from the drawing room. It's your older brother practising as part of his studies, as he does every morning. You're used to hearing the piano, but this sounds absolutely amazing. Your feet carry you to the drawing room and you find yourself mesmerised by the sound. You want to learn how to do that too.

You watch what he's doing: his fingers, his feet, his posture, his eyes. Your brother seems to be getting the information on how to do this from a piece of paper in front of him with dots and lines all over it. You've heard him discuss reading music with his teacher; although you haven't really thought about it much before, this must be what he's doing. If you want to be a part of this music-making malarkey, this is clearly the way to go.

Once he's finished, you ask him how you can learn to play that wonderful piece of music. He tells you that you'll need to learn to read it first. You'll happily follow his advice, because at this stage in the evolution of learning and playing music, it's absolutely true.

The traditional model of learning to play an instrument is there for a good reason and it hinges on this simple fact. In 1802, there weren't any recordings. If Beethoven wanted to be a rock star and write music for a living, he was going to have to get his music out to the wider world. Since he couldn't sell it on record, tape, CD or mp3, his only option was to write it down, take it to the printing press and get it published so that other people could play it.

Beethoven was the *composer*, and the people who played his music were the *performers*. The composer came up with the instructions and the performers followed them. There needed to be some common language to pass instructions from composers to performers, and that common language was written music.

People who created music needed to learn to write it, and people who played it needed to learn to read it. Since there was more opportunity to excel as a performer than a composer in a time when access to a printing press was unthinkably expensive, people based music education around learning to follow the instructions rather than write them. Read the music, play the notes then hear the result. Learning to read music first was a necessity and thus a priority. Budding musicians understood this and would be prepared to learn the process to get to the end result. It made sense.

This was the cool of 1802.

Then They Invented Recording

In 1857, Édouard-Léon Scott de Martinville invented the phonautograph, the first device capable of recording sound waves. It wasn't intended to replay the sounds, but it did capture them and represent them in visual form. In 1877, inventor extraordinaire Thomas Edison took it one stage further and built in playback ability to his invention, the phonograph. He tested it by recording and replaying 'Mary Had A Little Lamb'.

The problem with the phonograph was that while it could record and replay sounds, it couldn't reproduce them and send them to other machines to be played. This came ten years later in 1887 with the gramophone, invented by Emile Berliner.

It took a few decades for the technology to be picked up and used on a mass scale. The first pop star was arguably Enrico Caruso, who recorded songs for the Gramophone Company and made over a million pounds doing so. The first jazz artists started recording in 1917, and by 1940 a guitarist called Les Paul had figured out how to record different instruments at different times and put them on to one recording, known as multi-track. This was used in music studios widely in the 1960s, with The Beatles and The Rolling Stones being the first to make use of it in their recording.

By 1964, vinyl was the worldwide industry standard. Musicians were recording their songs in studios and pressing them on to vinyl. The record companies would then reproduce as many copies as the market demanded and ship them off for people to play on their vinyl players. This marked a significant shift in the way music was distributed. It was no longer in the written form and distributed via a printing press; it was now in audio form and distributed via vinyl.

The boundaries between performer and composer blurred and in many cases merged into one. Rock stars like Mick Jagger, Paul McCartney and Jimi Hendrix both composed their own songs and performed them. Becoming a rock star relied on you having abilities in both areas, and you no longer had to read or write music to get there. You simply needed to be able to play it.

From the perspective of music education, the switch is a little more subtle, which is perhaps why it's been missed, by and large. Before recorded music, things had to be done in a certain order. To hear the latest Beethoven or

Mozart piece, you first had to read and then play it. There was literally no other option.

Now, we get to hear the music first, which opens up the possibility of learning by ear.

Learning By Ear

Learning to play by ear is the art of hearing a piece of music and then copying it without seeing it written down. To start with, it can be a process of trial and error, but when a musician becomes modestly skilled at it, they will be able to listen to a song and play it almost straight away. Advanced players can do this even with very complex pieces of music, and have no trouble translating what they hear in their head directly on to their instrument. Many cultures who didn't go through the printing press era have always learned to play this way.

Sir Paul McCartney is an interesting example of someone who learned to play entirely by ear. The Beatles need no introduction. They changed the face of music as we know it today and brought the concept of a rock and pop band to mass appeal. They were considered some of the greatest composers and performers of all time, so it probably came as a bit of a surprise to many that Sir Paul didn't read or write music at all.

There's an interview on YouTube that explains both the situation and what the common reaction to it is:

Interviewer: You don't read music?

Paul: No, have you got a problem with that?

Interviewer: No, but it's quite amazing.

Paul: Well, you had to mention it in front of all these people!

Interviewer: You're one of the most successful songwriters of all time and you don't read music?

Paul: No. As long as the two of us, i.e. John and I, know what we're doing, we know what chords we're playing and we remember the melody, we don't ever actually have the need to write it down. Or to read it.

He's not alone. Jimi Hendrix, Elvis Presley, Eric Clapton, The Bee Gees, James Hetfield of Metallica, Thom Yorke of Radiohead, not to mention the obvious, –Stevie Wonder. These iconic musicians learned by figuring out how to play what they were hearing, not what they were seeing. What's interesting is the interviewer finds this 'amazing' when, for the majority of people, it's a far more natural learning process than reading.

You Don't Learn To Read Before You Learn To Speak

A good way to think about it is how we learn language. It's much more effective if we learn to speak it first than if we learn through reading or writing. This is, in fact, why children learn to speak naturally at a young age. Hearing sounds and then copying them is a very intuitive process. As you get better at this, you start to connect together the meanings of different words and learn to use them in the right order and the right context. Before too long, you're the master of your own words and are using them to express what you mean to others.

You learn to do all of this before you even go to school, and by the time you learn to read and write, you've already had a lot of practice in speaking. Can you imagine how slow the process of learning to speak would be if you had to recognise the word in written form before you were allowed to say it? How much longer would it take to build a vocabulary? How would you understand the meaning if your brain's processing power was being taken up with recognising the words? It would then be even more of a struggle to learn to write your own sentences and express yourself.

Let's compare this situation to learning to play an instrument. Music is a remarkably simple language. Western music has just twelve notes in it, and while these can be played in different orders or at the same time as each other, it's much like learning a language with twelve basic sounds or letters. It takes some time to translate this on to your instrument, but the learning process of recognising a sound, playing it and then checking whether it came out right is remarkably similar to speaking. By learning music as a language, we're tapping into something we already know how to do.

Then there's the expressive side. Much like people use speech to communicate, musicians today expect to be able to compose their own material to express themselves. Learning to do so through sight rather than sound is a very hard process indeed as it's a stage removed. Is it any wonder that most of our best songwriters today haven't taken this route?

So Why Learn To Read And Write Music At All Today?

Given that a lot of the best musicians of the last century didn't learn to play through writing or reading music, and it's a much harder way into it, why would we teach it at all?

It all comes down to your reasons for wanting to play (again!) in the first place. There are a small proportion of children who relate more to the composer/performer model and want to be performers. They would like to play in a wind band, an orchestra, or an ensemble where they follow the instructions in the written music and play it as well as they can. There is satisfaction in that for some, and if you want to be part of that music scene, there's no other way to get into it.

There are also some children who enjoy the process of learning to read music as they relate to it on a symbolic level. The way to find out if this is the right route for a child is, as ever, to ask them. If they're enthusiastic about the prospect of being a pure performer and playing this style of music, try it out and see how they respond.

For the majority of children learning an instrument today, however, it's a difficult and unnecessary barrier sitting between them and what they want to achieve. There are many more aspiring rock and pop musicians out there than there are classical performers. The songs they want to be able to play are often remarkably simple to start with, and the basics that enable them to learn these songs can be achieved very quickly. This allows them to focus on playing with other people and putting on concerts, achieving the social uplift they were motivated by in the first place. They get a boost in confidence and then go back for more. It's a wonderful upward spiral.

If you really are concerned about children learning to read music, then I suggest it is introduced after the child has learned the basics of playing in time, has a decent vocabulary of songs under their belt and has even composed a few of their own. This way, like learning to read and write at school after they've learned to speak, they're approaching things in the right order. Because continuing with the tradition of learning to read music from day one is having a whole host of unfavourable consequences for the majority of children.

Tread Carefully

When you put barriers up in learning, children believe it has to be hard. I've never yet met a person who doesn't want to do well in life, especially a child. They all start out by trying their best. But if they're confronted by something that's patently out of their reach, their efforts quickly turn into frustration.

If they've taken up music to be cool and impress their friends, introducing them to written music first puts that goal a long way in the distance. Confidence wavers as they continue to struggle on to the next level. They start protesting about learning an instrument at all. It becomes a chore, and they become that little bit less happy about themselves.

It doesn't have to be this way, and I don't believe it should be, which is why Rocksteady Music School is constantly on a mission to make music as simple and accessible as possible. By keeping it simple, we're increasing the number of opportunities to get those 'aha' moments for children in lessons. And it's through these moments that confidence is built.

PART 3
A GREAT REHEARSAL
FOR REAL LIFE

Chapter 7: Keep It Simple And Build Confidence

Chapter 8: Play Music With Others

Chapter 9: Playing Music For Others

Chapter 10: The Journey To Independence

In this section we'll be getting into the nitty gritty of how the Rocksteady method of teaching works, and more importantly, what it does for the children we teach.

In Chapter 7 we'll take an overview of how we introduce younger children to playing music and how it really is as simple as playing the right note at the right time.

In Chapter 8 we'll discover why playing music in a group where each person has their part accelerates learning, as well as tips for recreating this environment at home.

In Chapter 9 we'll discover why playing concerts for others is a vital part of the learning process, and in Chapter 10 we'll cover what Rocksteady lessons look like as the children progress, and how playing in a band can be a great opportunity to achieve something very meaningful indeed.

KEEP IT SIMPLE AND BUILD CONFIDENCE

In the last chapter we discussed the barriers inherent in learning to play the traditional way. In this chapter, we'll look at how to remove them and build confidence in playing music from the word go. What I'm about to tell you is simple, but stunningly effective. So much so that we've successfully taught thousands of children to play their instruments in a band using it.

The first and only step is to play the right notes at the right time.

Playing The Right Note At The Right Time

Emily and George turn up to their first lesson with Rocksteady. Emily has chosen guitar and George has chosen to play the drums. They have seen all of the instruments performed at the assembly workshop day and they're excited about playing in a band.

Today they are starting alongside five other children from different year groups who are playing keyboards, guitars and singing. Which song will they get to play?

Their band leader Tom welcomes them in and they settle down for a chat about what their band name is going to be. After a little deliberation about whether their name should involve jellyfish or tractors, they settle on Tyrannosaurus iPad. Congratulating them on picking an excellent name, Tom then asks what their favourite songs are and plays them a few simple ones to choose from on his phone.

They pick 'Best Day Of My Life' by The American Authors and go to their instruments. Tom stands in the middle where everyone can see him.

'Okay, George. As the drummer, it's your job to keep the beat. One of the drums you're going to be using to do that is the big one by your foot. I want you to play it at exactly the same time I clap my hands. Ready? One, two, three, four... clap.'

It takes a few attempts. The timing of the pedal is awkward, but within about twenty seconds, George can do it.

'Right, now we're going to keep counting to eight, and I want you to play it on every single number. Here we go – one, two, three, four, five, six, seven, eight. One, two, three, four... '

Tom continues, and George has to focus to get this right, but he's managing. Within a minute, George has learned to play in time with Tom's voice.

'That was awesome, George. You played at exactly the same time as I was counting. Good job.'

The objectives for the first time musician are all about playing simple patterns at the right time and listening to everyone else, but we don't need to tell them that. It gets in the way. We just say 'Hit that drum at exactly the same time as I clap.'

It's a similar story for the other musicians.

'Okay, Emily, you've got two notes to learn for this song. The first is called D. You play by pushing your finger down here and plucking the string.'

Tom points to the tenth fret on the low E string, but doesn't concern Emily with these details. She's got enough to concentrate on.

The first couple of attempts don't quite work.

'Okay, Emily, good effort. I want you to squeeze harder with that hand. Imagine you're trying to squeeze an orange.'

It works. The note D comes out.

'That's awesome, Emily! I'm going to count to eight again, except instead of one, I'm going to say D. I want you to play D every time I say it at exactly the same time. Ready? D, two, three, four, five, six, seven, eight. D, two, three, four, five, six, seven, eight...'

Tom repeats a similar exercise with the keyboard players, while the singer sings the word D and helps with counting to eight. After five minutes they're ready to have a go at playing music as a band.

'Right, everyone, we're going to try and play the first note in the song as a band. The important thing is to play the D at exactly the same time. George, you have to play on all the numbers too, okay? Ready everyone? One, two, three, four... '

Tom then launches into calling out 'D, two, three, four, five, six, seven, eight' and clapping along for the next minute while the band play along with him. It doesn't go perfectly at first. There are some children playing the right note at not quite the right time and others have drifted on to different notes, but he coaches them through it. After five minutes of continuous rehearsal, they're starting to sound pretty good.

They repeat the process with G, the second note in the song. The children pick it up quicker this time, so after a few rounds they're ready to try both together. This stage is altogether trickier so Tom offers them some tips.

'The song is going to go: D, two, three, four, five, six, seven, eight; G, two, three, four, five, six, seven, eight, over and over again. After you've played your D, look at where your G is and get ready in your head to move to it. After you've played your G, look straight back at your D, but wait until I say it before you play it. George, you keep watching my hands clapping to make sure you play the drum at exactly the right time. Everyone ready?'

It doesn't go smoothly the first few times. Tom stops play each time and gently reminds them that the notes have to be played at exactly the right time. The children pick up on the message – this is important to Tom, so it must be important to them too.

The vocalist is taught the chorus and, with encouragement from Tom, sings it over the top of all the Ds and Gs.

After a little more practice it starts to gel, and the children relax as they're playing it. There are still looks of intense concentration, but they're also smiling. They're playing a song they've heard on the radio and they're doing it well. It took them half an hour to learn two notes, which is not a world apart from the output of a traditional music lesson, but this *feels* radically different. They're playing in a band with their peers and learning from someone who plays in a real band themselves. They can feel the energy in the room.

They think about the experience throughout the week and look forward to the next one. It was awesome and they can't wait to do it again. As they relive it, they're playing D and G over in their heads. George is tapping his foot and counting to eight in the car on the way home. The children all show up to the next session raring to go.

And this is the basis of the Rocksteady method. There's a lot more subtlety to it as the children develop their musical skills, but there's always an emphasis on teaching them in the most simple, direct way possible.

There Are No Wrong Notes In Music

Things don't always go so smoothly. Like learning any new skill, there are obstacles to overcome. There are times when your fingers won't do what your brain is telling them to. Or there's the reverse, where that switch between notes makes your brain freeze. You make a mistake, maybe once or maybe many times. These situations can be stressful, especially in front of your role model and a group of peers.

The key is to make sure that mistakes are completely nor-malised in band practices and at concerts.

What do I mean by normalising mistakes? Well, it's one thing to say that it's okay to make mistakes, it's another altogether to make them routine – an expected part of learning. Quite often in modern life, and especially in education, we put ourselves into a performance environment rather than a learning environment. In situations where we have a limited amount of time to produce a result, like a job interview or, indeed, a music exam, this makes sense. We are there to perform and mistakes are generally frowned upon. But you can take this one stage further and simulate the performance environment while you're learning in order to train yourself in managing the feelings a performance environment brings about. This is very common in education – we do mock exams from an early age. The question is always 'Did you succeed?' and it's a yes or no answer.

It works to an extent, but I think it's important not to take performance environments too far. The learning environment, by contrast, celebrates mistakes, because it's through making them that you learn. Much like you can simulate a performance environment while learning, you can also simulate a learning environment while performing if you create a safe enough space.

Rocksteady concerts are a perfect example. We put bands through them regardless of whether they've got their songs perfect or not. We set up the appropriate expectations for the audience as to what each individual band should be getting out of the concert, and then praise the bands for their courage in making an effort.

Another good example of a learning environment is how you responded to your child when they were learning to speak. They frequently made mistakes in their grammar and pronunciation, and sometimes got their words mixed up altogether. You helped them out by correcting them, but the tone of your voice was very encouraging and you celebrated every time they made an effort.

We do the same thing when we're teaching children to play in bands. Once children know they can mess it up entirely and actually be praised for their efforts, they're not afraid to give things as many try's as are needed to get it right.

Honestly, There Are No Wrong Notes In Music

This message can be harder for some children to accept than others. Jordan is an eight-year-old drummer from a small school in the Hampshire countryside. He cries on a daily basis, not just in his music lessons, but in all sorts of situations. When he's taught a new drum beat, he gives it a go until he makes a mistake. Then he stops, his head drops and he looks very sad.

'Let's give it another go,' says his band leader, Richard.

'But I'm going to fail,' Jordan replies, clearly upset.

'It doesn't matter if you make mistakes, I make mistakes all the time...'

Jordan cuts Richard off. 'I am going to FAIL!'

The other children look concerned. You could cut the atmosphere with a knife. They go ahead anyway for the sake of the rest of the band, but it lasts around five seconds before Jordan misses a beat, throws his sticks on the floor and starts crying. This scene plays itself out every week.

'We tried everything,' explains Richard. 'I demonstrated mistakes myself, the rest of the band helped by pointing out their mistakes and laughing about them, I said time and time again that I only cared about whether he tried, not whether he could do it, but he didn't believe me. He saw it as a very black and white thing. Make a mistake and you're a failure.'

But this all changed when Madonna made one of the most famous slip-ups of her career. Literally. She was performing at the 2015 Brit Awards when someone stepped on her outfit and she was pulled to the floor, flat on her back, from the top of a set of stairs. Like any true performer, she got back up and carried on, and in doing so provided Richard with a tremendous opportunity.

'As soon as I saw that I thought of Jordan and told him go home and watch it on YouTube. I explained that Madonna had made a mistake on a massive level in front of millions of people and told him to look at how the crowd responded – she got a far bigger cheer than she would have had it not happened. And she got the cheer because she got up and continued.'

Jordan went home and watched the video and it changed his life. He's still working on feeling totally comfortable with getting things wrong, but he hasn't cried in lessons for six months now, and that's a major step forward for him. At the time of writing, there's a push towards building strength of character in the British education system, and with good reason. Having the resilience to get up and try again when things go wrong is a skill that improves our lives immeasurably; none of us can do without it. When we learn to see mistakes as setbacks rather than failures, we give ourselves the space to keep practising and make progress towards our goals. For a child like Jordan, that's going to take some time, but thanks to the opportunity to play in a band, Richard's insight and Madonna's slip up, he's well on his way.

Counting To 100... Games Are Fun

Learning a new skill involves a lot of repetition. There's no getting around it, especially during the early stages when basic notes and simple movement patterns are the goal. Playing in time, too, is an art form that eventually becomes natural, but only after many hours of doing it. That's why we put a big emphasis on spending the whole time playing the song in lessons. Still, the fun can get sapped out of playing the same two notes over and over again, so we spice it up with an arsenal of games that give playing a new angle and make it fun.

One such game came to me when I was teaching a band of four- and five-year-olds who wanted to play 'Firework' by Katy Perry. Even a very basic version of 'Firework' has four notes in it, and I had to find a way of getting them to play these notes in time with each other as many times as possible to imbed them in their brains. The drummer had two different movement patterns to master, the kick drum and hi-hat at the same time (which we called feet) and the snare drum and hi-hat together (which we called hands).

I started as I usually do:

'Okay, after four I'd like our drummer to play "feet" and everybody else in the band to a play an A. One, two, three, four, A!'

After a few goes at that, we moved on to playing A twice.

'One, two, three, four, A, A.'

Then four times.

'One, two, three, four, A, A, A, A.'

Then, struck with a moment of inspiration, I asked the drummer what his favourite number was. After some deliberation and counting of fingers, we concluded it was seven.

'Right then, we're going to play A seven times!'

It took a couple more children to volunteer their favourite numbers before the joker of the band spotted a way to make this game a lot more fun.

'A hundred!' he said with a big grin on his face.

Brilliant. 'Okay, we're going to play this note a hundred times!'

Everyone laughed their way through it before the next child piped up with 200. By the end of the game (which lasted all lesson) we'd played all four notes in time, thousands of times.

We use this game, and many others like it, to keep the learning fun. The goal is to play a song at a concert, but there are a variety of ways to get there, and there's no reason to make rehearsals boring.

Songs, The Rocket Fuel Behind Progression

When we were learning to speak, we did so by picking up phrases from the adults around us and copying them. My niece Cora is eleven months old at the time of writing and is just about forming her first words, her favourites being the phrase: 'Who's that?' She says it all the time, and mostly in context – when she hears someone coming into a room or the phone rings.

Her dad told me this didn't happen by design. They were in the car together one day when the phone rang, and he innocently said, 'Who's that?' to hear Cora repeat it back to him in a flash. She's been using it ever since.

Cora's ability to speak will emerge gradually as she picks up more phrases from different people and starts piecing them together. A linguist friend of mine tells me that once children have fifty words under their belts, they start connecting them and progress becomes rapid.

Now, there are only twelve notes in music so it's not quite such a complex task as learning a language, but there are an infinite number of ways of playing them. Just like learning a language, you need to get to grips with why they work together in certain patterns. And what better way to do this than by learning how musicians that inspire you have been using them?

The traditional approach to learning the full range of notes an instrument has on it is by learning scales. For example, a G major scale has G, A, B, C, D, E and F sharp in it. This is all very well and good, but when the notes are out of context, you're not going to get to that critical point where you understand how to connect them. It would be like learning to speak by starting with the alphabet.

Consider instead starting with songs. 'Shine Bright Like A Diamond' by Rhianna has G, A and B in it. When you play them in the song, you can feel what the song is trying to say with them. You learn that those three notes, played in a specific order, will have that effect.

'I'm Yours' by Jason Mraz can be played using G, D, E and C. We can learn to play 'One Way Or Another' using G, F# and E. By the time you've learned those, you understand how to use the notes in a G major scale. Through experience and repetition, you build confidence and an awareness of how to use the language of music quite organically. From this point, progress rockets as your brain starts making more and more connections and you absorb new songs more easily.

Then one day, you hear a song and just know how to play it. By that point you've truly learned how to play by ear. You're no longer dependent on sheet music to tell you what to do as a musician. You've built a skill that you can enjoy time and time again throughout your life. And nothing is more enjoyable than sharing it with other people.

PLAY MUSIC WITH OTHERS

Brooke plays in a band called The Dirty Pigs (and why not?). She's nine years old, a sporty child who has a lot of confidence. Her mum, Paula, ferries her and her friends to and from school, and their band often comes up in conversation. Who's going to do what on stage? Which song are they going to play next? Should Brooke stay on the keyboard or is she more suited to singing? Each issue is pushed, pulled and debated at length.

By comparison, Brooke's involvement in the choir and recorder lessons produces less of a stir. She's got a concert tomorrow where she's singing in the choir. The sheet of music has been on the kitchen side waiting for her to practise for several weeks now and hasn't been picked up once.

Ownership = Results

Discussions about what needs to be done, who's going to do it and how to get it done are part of band life. Heck, they're part of life full stop! At Rocksteady, we feel learning how to handle them is an essential part of developing into a happy, capable and confident adult. As such, we actively use some of the time in rehearsals to encourage these sorts of conversations by asking the right questions and then standing back.

One of my favourite questions after a band has got to grips with their parts is 'How would you like it to end?' The conversation usually unfolds something like this:

'Can we have a fadeout for the ending?'

'How would a fadeout even work when we're playing at a concert?'

'I'm not sure. Maybe we could ask our friends to turn the volume down on the amplifier?'

'That could work. My friend James will do it!'

'No, I'm not sure we want extra people on stage.'

'That's true. Well, could Paul (the singer) do it? He's finished his parts by then.'

'I could give it a go. How do I do it?'

These discussions show two things. First of all, the children really care about what they're doing. They feel like they own their work and have personal responsibility for what they show the world. Secondly, they're learning about more than just playing their instruments. They're learning about the social dynamics of achieving something in a team.

Brooke's mum Paula explains, 'It's all about being part of something they own. The fact that they're arguing over who's singing in the next concert show's how much pride they're taking in it. It's healthy.'

And indeed it is. My first forays into forming a band as a teenager taught me how to recruit people and get them riled up about what we were doing. I learned how to deal with issues as they arose, work with strong personalities, and even how to bounce back from being kicked out of a band I had started! It wasn't always easy, but I took a lot from it, and it's a big part of what's allowed me to set up and run companies as an adult.

Learning these soft skills early in life with a role model there to support your development is all valuable experience.

Team Sports

The benefits of team sports for children are well documented. In addition to being a fun way of staying physically healthy, one of the main perks of getting involved with your local football, rugby or netball club is that your child learns to work with others. If they're to be successful, they'll need to learn to balance their individual thinking with thinking as a group. They learn respect and empathy for others, and they see the benefits of organisation and practice come to fruition in something that they care about. For some, it is also their route into other essential life skills such as discipline, persistence, resilience and confidence.

Playing in a band is similar in many ways. You're working with a group of peers towards a common goal. With team sports it's winning a game and beating the other team; with music it's usually playing a concert or recording your songs. Like sport, you have to learn to balance your individual thinking with what's best for the group, something that isn't always emphasised in the academic side of school. You also get to experience the benefits of your practice, discipline and persistence.

The way in which the two differ is that sport operates within a predefined set of rules that both teams have to work to. With music, there are no rules. Really, there aren't. You can do whatever you want.

I used to start each school year with a talk to the children:

'There are no rules in music. If it sounds good to you, then it is good. If it doesn't, then it isn't. You might love the sound of someone banging their forks on the table, or a group of people gurgling water in time with each other. It might be the best thing you've ever heard. What one person thinks is good may not be the same for the next person. It's all about how you feel.'

Music is completely subjective, which is why we have so many different styles in the world, ranging from the common rock and pop genres to dance, heavy metal, jazz and avant-garde minimalist music. This freedom to go in whichever direction you want attracts some children. I remember one ten-year-old keyboard player getting particularly excited when his band agreed to make Rhianna's 'Shine Bright Like A Diamond' more to his tastes by playing the chorus in a Norwegian death metal style.

To navigate such freedom, however, requires quite a different set of social skills than the stricter framework sports bring. In sport you may discuss how best to position the players and negotiate specific tactics for winning against a particular team. When playing in a band, you have to learn to do a bit more blue sky thinking before you even get to the stage. What should we call ourselves? What should we play? What sort of band are we going to be? At least when we were playing rounders we could all agree that we were here to win. What are we even trying to show the world here?

For five- and six-year-olds, these sorts of issues are usually quite mild. They're just excited about learning to play and getting to be a rock star. But for older children it can be more serious business. Sit with a group of nine- and ten-year-olds trying to decide their band name and you'll see it in action.

I remember teaching a band called Crossbow, which consisted of three headstrong boys and three equally headstrong girls all aged between nine and eleven. We were deciding which songs to play, listening through my playlist on Spotify, when we came across a heavy metal song by Metallica.

The boys and one of the girls were instantly enthusiastic. 'Let's do this one! Yes! Please! Please!'

The keyboard player from the band was more curious than enthusiastic, but the singer wasn't at all convinced. I watched her think as the rest of the band jumped on persuading her that this was the song for them. I could see her picturing herself singing this song on stage in her head. Was this something she could do? Would she want to be seen singing this song?

She didn't say anything. The rest of the group looked at me.

'Can we, please?'

'It's up to *all* of you. If your singer doesn't think this song is right for her then you'll have to think about what that would mean for your concert. Talk about it and figure it out.'

'Can we listen to it again from the beginning?' asked the singer.

I played it again. This time everyone was not just listening for themselves, but also for their singer. They each looked around the group intently, trying to figure out how to play it. The singer looked at everyone and took in how excited they were. A smile came across her face halfway through.

'We'll do it!'

At the concert that Christmas, they played the song fantastically. The singer sang it with confidence and passion, knowing she had the whole band behind her. The head teacher then asked the audience to cheer the loudest for whichever band they wanted to do an encore. They cheered for Crossbow. Metallica turned out to be a great group decision for them.

Levelling The Playing Field

Owen is ten years old and has severe dyslexia. As a result, he struggles with academic subjects and requires a learning assistant with him during lessons at school. Most days, he's taken out to do extra session on literacy and numeracy to catch up. His school day is different from the other children and he's acutely aware of it, to the point that he's developed a negative set of beliefs around learning. The words 'I can't' are a staple in his vocabulary.

When he started playing the drums with Rocksteady, he had lessons by himself. He frequently had a similar reaction to Jordan when he made a mistake: his head dropped into his hands and he'd throw his drum sticks down.

'I can't do it,' he said, time and time again.

His band leader, Mike, picked up a guitar and started jamming with him.

'I used to make mistakes myself deliberately, all over the place, and that helped him somewhat, but the game really changed for him when others joined his band.'

Suddenly he was on a level playing field. Mike explains.

'It worked out quite differently for Owen. When there were four other children working towards the same thing as him and he had no special attention, he realised that he wasn't that different from anyone else. He had to play his part on the drums for the sake of the whole group. He felt empowered and started showing determination when he faced a setback.'

Things really changed when Owen played his first concert at school alongside the rest of his band.

'Previously, Owen was concerned that his peers saw him as the one who always needed help, yet here he was, an equal with the rest of his band, playing music for everyone in the school. His attitude around who he was and what he was capable of started to shift that day.'

His mum Dorothy tells us that this phase of Owen's life really turned things around for him.

'He started to look forward to school on Rocksteady days, and after that first concert his confidence changed altogether. In Year 3 and 4 he had refused to do any school plays or take part in class assemblies. Since Rocksteady he's had no problem at all, and doesn't mind giving anything a go, even if he might not succeed first time.'

Learning to play in a band was a relatively simple intervention, but a powerful one. Sometimes it's not about standing out as an individual, but having your part to play and being on the same level as everyone else. It certainly worked for Owen.

Peer Pressure

When I first started teaching bands at Northern Parade, until that point I'd only been teaching one instrument at a time. If the pupils were learning guitar, it would be in a guitar lesson. Generally speaking, a one on one lesson would deliver more benefit than a two pupils to one teacher situation. Two would be better than three, etc. Under this model, the more attention each pupil can receive, the better their progression is likely to be.

Given this, my expectations weren't exactly high when I first attempted to teach eight children different instruments at the same time.

The results surprised me, to say the least.

It was slower going at first, but definitely more effective. There seemed to be something about each member having their own part, different from anybody else in the band, that made them more serious about learning it. The levels of concentration in the room were much higher than I'd previously seen in group lessons. Once the basics of playing in time were in place, progress for all members of the band skyrocketed.

It was as if playing their parts with other people from their peer group helped the skills bed in on a much deeper level than playing them with their teacher. In small group guitar lessons, it always seemed up to me to create the momentum as we tried to progress on to more challenging things. When the children were learning as a band, they generated the momentum all by themselves.

So what was going on here? I'll be the first to admit I'm not sure of the science behind it, but it seems to have something to do with peer pressure. Now, we often hear of peer pressure in a negative context as the reason a child's chosen to partake in some sort of undesirable behaviour, but it can also be a positive thing.

When we were learning 'Seven Nation Army' with Harry's band, it was his job to start the song on the bass guitar. The drummer, Joao, then had to come in with a drum rhythm that would provide the build-up for the song. If he didn't bring the right parts in at the right time throughout the verse, pre chorus and chorus, it would throw the rest of the group off. If they didn't listen to each other and play together, the singer wouldn't know where to begin and wouldn't have the basis she needed to front the band. When the chorus came in, it was the guitar and keyboard players' job to make it sound huge. They had to be aware of what everyone else was doing and when it was their turn to come in. They needed to be ready at exactly the right time and then start playing in sync with the drums and bass.

Each child relied on every other band member to pull the song together. They didn't want to be the one to let the group down. When children feel this level of responsibility and know it's on them to play their part, the level of concentration goes up to another level and they're that much more able to learn. What's more, after a few rehearsals they would be playing this song in front of the school, so they needed to play it well to impress. It's peer pressure all round, but it's the right sort of peer pressure because it's directed towards a positive outcome for something the children want to do. It's the sort of peer pressure that builds confidence rather than destroys it.

Working Towards A Goal

There's a tremendous sense of achievement that comes from working towards a common goal with a group of people. The saying goes: 'If you want to go fast, go alone; if you want to go far, go together'. Many of Rocksteady's band leaders say that they've met most of their friends and acquaintances through music. Richard Bushby, whose teaching is featured a lot in this book, says that his entire friendship group, his wife and his work have all come through music:

'In fact, anything of any significance that wasn't my family.'

It's like being part of any group that does something important for other people. You get to make them smile, dance and generally get excited to see what you've been up to. Most bands the world over attract a fan culture for this reason. It's really quite a journey, and a big part of that journey is playing for other people, which is why the next chapter is all about playing gigs.

Can Music Really Be Learned In This Way?

As I said, I was as surprised as anyone with the progress that children made under this method. But what exactly do I mean by progress? Well, in this case I mean developing the ability to play songs on your instrument, with other people and to an audience. I mean gaining an understanding of how music is put together, about how songs are written and where each part sits. I mean developing an awareness of which parts to play and how they fit into the greater whole. These skills are practical, transferable between all instruments and form the basis of playing with others in a band.

And to these ends, learning in a band works better than any other type of lesson I've ever seen. To me, these are foundations of playing and appreciating music that will set you up for life.

One area aside from reading music that we don't emphasise at Rocksteady is achieving technical brilliance. By technical brilliance, I mean the physical abilities needed to play some of the more challenging music out there in the world. To play a guitar solo by Jimi Hendrix, you'll need to master a variety of specific techniques, from bending the strings to playing with one hand to learning how to control the sound using effects pedals. To play the introduction to 'I Will Survive' on the keyboard, you'll need to be able to race through arpeggios across multiple octaves. To be able to play the introduction to The Arctic Monkeys' 'I Bet You Look Good On The Dancefloor' on the drums, you'll need to be able to fit quick drum fills into the middle of a beat.

Children gain an awareness of these things in Rocksteady lessons simply by being exposed to more music and learning from their band leaders (who can do these things), but the technical requirements for playing more challenging pieces don't usually get covered in a band rehearsal environment. They require quite specific work and somebody who is a specialist in that instrument to show you the nuances. Your child may or may not want to take their instrument to that sort of technical level, but if they do, then I always recommend a good private teacher to support them on that particular journey.

Where Does This Leave Practice At Home?

The simple answer is that practice at home is *not required* to do well using this method. I've seen it work fantastically well for children who don't have any instruments to practise on, so practice is certainly not compulsory. The social pressure, the team element, the sense of ownership and the increased mental engagement in and out of lessons seem to do the trick. But just because it's not required, it doesn't mean that playing an instrument outside of lessons isn't going to be helpful, especially for children who want to make sure they've got it right for their rehearsal or concert next week.

A common problem to watch out for is that the home environment is very different to playing in a band with friends and can get stale after a while. The trick is to make sure it is *playing* that they're doing rather than *practice*. If you want to help, here are some do's, don'ts and suggestions to get you started:

1. Use the word play, not practice.

Practice: *repeated performance of systematic exercise for the purpose of acquiring skill or proficiency.*

Play: *exercise or activity for amusement or recreation.*

Which sounds like something you would have liked to do after a day at school? Especially after that mountain of homework has been climbed. Your child may not be able to reel off the dictionary definition, but they do understand the difference between the two. So make a conscious effort to use the word play instead of practice. It's a lot more rewarding *and* effective for both parent and child.

2. Ask them to play a concert for you.

The concert can be for just you, their siblings, or all your friends and family at a summer BBQ. Some children love playing in front of others and learn a lot from the sensation and feedback they get from an audience. Your child may be one of them, and if this turns out to be the case, get them to stand on their bed (the stage!), crowd into their room, dim the lights and cheer like you mean it. It's also worth noting that a lot is learned in the preparation for the concert too, so the more effort that goes into it from both you and your child, the better.

3. Ask them to teach you.

Asking your child to teach you their instrument is another great way of getting them to share their new found skills. When they teach someone else, they get clear on exactly what it is they know. If your child loves communicating and being helpful, this could be the one for them. It may take time to start being productive, but if you persist and turn it into a regular event, especially on the day of their lessons, you'll see the fruits of your labour before too long.

4. Have a jam.

Get out the pots and pans, old keyboards, download an instrumental app on your phone and try things out together. For those children who learn by exploring, this can be an excellent method of sharing in their journey. Focus on keeping some sort of steady rhythm, encourage listening to each other and ask your child for suggestions as you go. You may be amazed at what comes out of it. This can be combined with your child teaching you new skills or the concert option for even more fun.

5. Challenge your child.

This is a method to tread carefully with, but asking 'Do you reckon you could do X?' works particularly well for children who thrive on a challenge. If your child comes home having learned C, A, G and F, ask them if they could play them in a different order. Could they play each of them four times, eight times, forty times? Could they write their own song?

If they come home with a drum beat, could they play it faster? Could they play it really slowly? Could they play it for two minutes without stopping?

If they're learning to sing a song, could they write a new verse or change some of the words to make it their own?

If your child responds well to this, be sure to praise their effort by saying something along the lines of 'I'm impressed with how you got stuck in and tried it' whether or not they got the desired result. Also be sure to ask them what they learned afterwards. Be creative as you like and have fun with it.

6. Ask them to explain it to you.

'How does that work?' is a great question for analytical children. Whether it's explaining how a verse and chorus go together, showing you how they line up their fingers to find the next note or how to co-ordinate their limbs, they will love breaking it down and showing you how the music works. Asking the question 'How?' can really help them unlock what they know and learn it on a deeper level.

The key is to try a few of these activities and then observe you child's responses to them. Different things work for different children. Once you've got a good idea of what your child enjoys, keep the ones that work and throw out the rest.

9

PLAYING MUSIC FOR OTHERS

Life Defining Moments

Grace was a new face at her school in the leafy suburbs of Surrey. A quiet girl, she had moved down from East Anglia with her family in Year 5 when her dad's work relocated. She was having a hard time fitting in at her new school, and even as the new singer in her Rocksteady band, she was struggling to make her voice heard.

While working towards the Easter Concert, band leader Richard asked Grace what she would like to do during the parts of the song when she wasn't singing.

'I could clap my hands above my head and try to get people to clap along,' she suggested.

'Brilliant,' said Richard. 'Let's practise that in rehearsal so it's natural at the concert.'

It just so happened that the concert fell on Grace's tenth birthday. The band were their usual mix of nerves and excitement, and Grace was quiet. They were the last band to play, so nerves either had time to settle or build depending on the child. For Grace, they seemed to sit motionless.

After all the other bands had played, Grace's band was called to the stage. The early parts went past in a blur until she reached the appointed time, just before the final chorus. Grace started clapping above her head. The plan worked: all 330 children, every teacher and every parent in the audience started clapping along with her. She finished her final chorus to see the whole school erupt into applause and she smiled, knowing she'd just won the acceptance of the rest of the school in a big way.

Richard was beaming with pride. 'At the very least, she's going to remember that forever. At the most, it's probably fair to say that was a life defining moment for her.'

These sorts of things happen all the time when children are given an opportunity to perform. At Rocksteady, we could write whole books on the number of times we've seen it happen. Winning the acceptance of your peers is a big deal for any child; we saw it back in Chapter 3 with the hierarchy of needs. Playing in a band is the first step on the musical variation of this ladder, but playing to the whole school takes it up a notch.

For some children, this can feel like they've finally found their thing. Not everyone finds themselves winning popularity contests through sports, academic subjects or a naturally magnetic personality. We all express ourselves in different ways, and for some, music is their path. They gain acceptance through showing it to the world.

Nerves

But it's not just for those who are struggling to find their way through school life. I've yet to meet a child who hasn't benefited in some way. One of the many benefits of performing is it teaches children to manage their emotions. Getting up in front of a lot of people is a big deal. Those of us who have given presentations at work, delivered assemblies at school or even stood up to say a few words at a wedding will know all about this! It's like walking a tightrope between feeling excited and scared to death – incredibly exhilarating and nerve racking all at the same time.

Some fall more on the side of excitement and some fall more on the side of nerves. Even seasoned performers Adele, Ozzy Osbourne and Katy Perry have all confessed to dealing with pre-concert nerves. It's perfectly natural. We're hardwired to worry about our reputation, it's part of being human. What's more, it's the primitive parts of our brain that we have very little control over that are doing the worrying here. Adrenaline surges as a result, our senses heighten, our mouths dry up, we shake. We get butterflies. In Chapter 1, Jack from the Lightning Beasts described the feeling perfectly as 'butterflies dancing in my stomach'. That's his digestive system shutting down, getting ready for the danger his mind is dreaming up.

Learning to manage these butterflies is an essential part of growing into a confident adult. For children, the stakes can feel pretty high the first time they step on stage with their own band, so it helps if their early experiences are positive ones in a supportive environment. It also helps if they start experiencing these things at an early age. The old adage of practice making perfect may not be true, but it certainly makes things better.[1]

'What If I Make A Mistake?'

This is the most common concern from children about to get up and play in front of others. It's one thing to normalise making mistakes and learning in front of your band mates, it's another altogether to be comfortable with them in front of an audience.

I remember a conversation with one of our most experienced

---

[1] When I was younger I remember a lot of people telling me that practice makes perfect. It was my Judo instructor who put that right. 'Practice doesn't make you perfect, but it makes you better.' It stuck with me. The power of positive mentors in action.

Year 6 pupils before a concert.

'Is everything okay, Harrison?'

'Yeah,' (his body language was telling me he really meant no) 'I'm just worried that I'll mess up the singing or the drums. It's nearly impossible to do both at the same time.'

Harrison was a Rocksteady veteran. He had played guitar and drums in concerts many times over the last few years, but this was his first go at singing at the same time.

I dug a little deeper.

'Which bit are you most worried about?'

'The whole thing.'

'What do you think might happen?'

'Well if I make a mistake, everyone will know and then they'll laugh at me.'

That pretty much sums it up for a lot of children. There's pressure around getting it right. And the funny thing is, it's often misplaced.

I continued the chat.

'Ah, okay. I've played a lot of concerts before – I did two over the weekend. How many mistakes do you think I make when I play a concert?'

'None!'

'Guess again.'

'Maybe one or two?'

'Probably about 100 or maybe 200 in a whole gig.'

'Really?'

He looked sceptical.

'Yep, and how many people in the audience do you think know about it?'

'All of them?'

'Well no, not really. Probably a couple notice, but they don't mind.'

'Why not?'

'Well, why do you think people come to see a band play?'

'To have a good time and hear songs they know.'

'Exactly. Does the odd mistake stop them having fun or mean they can't recognise the song?'

'No, I guess not.'

'So what should we focus on to make sure they have fun?'

'Ummm, not sure.'

'Well, if you look like you're having a good time, it's a lot more likely the audience will have fun. Then you can all have fun together and nobody will notice a couple of mistakes.'

'Okay...'

He was still sceptical. I suspect he thought I was making it up to make him feel better. The funny thing is, I wasn't at all. Most musicians I know genuinely do make a whole host of mistakes during a performance. So why is there such a pressure around getting it right?

As we've already discussed, performing is stressful because we feel like we're being judged. Adults often feel it too. If that deep unconscious part of your brain is telling you that your reputation is at stake and the adult in the room is stressing the importance of getting it right, or, heaven forbid, perfect (because they feel their reputation somehow relies on that), the resulting pressure is enough to make any child feel sick.

It's not just performing on stage either, it's baked into the culture of how we reward and praise children through education. Leaving school tests and exams aside, music lessons have had their own traditions in this space which are not too dissimilar from exams in their atmosphere.

In these situations, you're assessed on how close to 'perfect' you perform on the day. The question is, is it necessary and is it doing our children any good?

Mrs Becket

I was lucky enough to have a teacher called Mrs Becket in primary school, and I did my first school Christmas play under her guidance. My part was to be an MC, stand up on a platform in a sparkly gold waistcoat and entertain the audience in between the staged acts. I was given a script for jokes to tell and things to say, but I had my own ideas too.

Rather than insist I do everything by the book, Mrs Becket listened to me and gave me full encouragement to try different things during rehearsals and performances to see what happened. I 'screwed up', got lost regularly and saw the audience still reacting positively. Mrs Becket supported me, even when it went wrong, so I improved each time and grew in confidence. This environment, where you feel that your teacher and audience are on your side rather than trying to catch you out, is absolutely essential to long term confidence. As a learning experience, it was worth more to my performing and teaching career than any amount of reciting lines or insisting on perfection.

It's not that getting it right doesn't matter, it's just that there are a lot of other things that matter more.

I introduced Harrison's band at the concert.

'Okay everyone, remember we give every band a big cheer as they come on stage and after they've finished the song.

'We have a very special act for you next. They've been working on listening to each other and playing as a team, but
they're also trying something new. Our drummer Harrison
decided at the beginning of the year that he would add to
the band's awesomeness by singing as well as playing the
drums. It's tricky to play the drums, it's tricky to sing, and it's
tricky to perform in front of everyone. Harrison's doing all
three at the same time, and the rest of his band are behind
him. Let's give them an extra massive cheer as they come
on stage.'

Harrison played the song as focused as I'd ever seen
him. He made a few mistakes, but they didn't matter. The
audience weren't looking for perfection, they were there to
support him.

Two minutes later, he was looking out over a cheering
audience and smiling. As he walked off the stage and sat
down, his body flopped with exhaustion. His head fell into
his hands as his adrenaline levels settled down. He took a
few moments to gather himself.

When he looked up, he was still smiling.

Tianna From Leopard Clone Wars

At the other end of the primary school age spectrum is
Tianna, the singer from Leopard Clone Wars. Tianna was

just five years old when she started learning how to sing in a band, and while she enjoyed the rehearsals, she used to cry and refuse to sing on stage whenever it came to concert time.

Her mum Amy explains that she had a negative experience at an early age.

'She sang a song in a school assembly, but when she'd finished, the backing track carried on. You could see the fear in her eyes. She lost her nerve for performing and struggled to remember the words.'

Amy wanted Tianna to overcome her nerves, but was concerned not to push her daughter too far at such a young age if it wasn't right for her.

'I often asked myself if I was doing the right thing, but sometimes you have to fall over in life to move forward.'

Amy spoke to Tianna's band leader Luke and they hatched a plan.

'We'd practise everything that could go wrong during rehearsals,' explains Luke. 'And I mean everything. We'd practise what would happen if the microphone stopped working. We practised tripping up walking on and off stage. We all made mistakes and totally derailed the song, but we kept going regardless.'

At home, Amy and Tianna made videos of her singing the song and watched them back, building her confidence one rehearsal and one video at a time.

For Tianna's next performance, her mum sat on stage with her. The crowd gave her a massive cheer and she understood, for the first time, that they were on her side. For her second concert six months later, Tianna stepped up to the microphone on her own and gave such a moving performance that her classroom teacher was the one crying this time.

Luke describes the scene. 'That was what really did it for Tianna. She looked up to her teacher so much, and when she saw that she had the ability to move her to tears, all the nerves went away and were replaced with something much more powerful. She'd learned to look past making mistakes and gained the confidence to stand up in front of any crowd.'

And stand up in front of crowds she did. A year later, when she sang 'Firework' on stage in front of several thousand people at the Guildhall, I would never have known this child had doubted herself for one second. Through the support of her teacher, her mum and Luke, Tianna had learned to overcome her nerves and developed a bravery that will stay with her for life.

Back To Progress

Performing is a wondrous enhancer for progress. It's like adding a booster switch. When I was younger, I remember an experienced musician telling me that you learn as much in one gig as ten rehearsals. He was right. For me, my progress went through the roof when my dad took me to local jam sessions every Monday night. Not only did I get to play with more experienced musicians, but crucially, I got to play to an audience.

I remember hearing a story from a man whose teacher used to encourage him to imagine he was playing the Royal Albert Hall each time he practised. He would close his eyes and put himself on stage there, and as a result found himself in a much better state for learning.

And it works. Just imagine you're standing with your instrument in front of several thousand people. Feel your breathing change and the hairs on the back of your neck stand up.

When you do something in front of other people and put yourself into a state of nerves and excitement, everything is magnified. Every emotion is felt more strongly, everything that goes right is absorbed on a deep level. Every mistake is a crucial learning experience.

Brooke's mum Paula described it as 'concentration like

she's never seen before', and that's pretty accurate in the early days of performing. As a result, when children come back to rehearsal afterwards, they're showing up with a deeper level of experience and desire to learn than before.

Why does this happen? I haven't done any formal research, but in my experience it's an extension of the social pressure theories from the last chapter. You learn faster when you're among five or six of your friends because you want to do well for the group. When you're performing for hundreds or even thousands of people, you multiply that effect and concentrate it into a few minutes. Much like playing a match in tennis, or taking part in a race if you're a runner, this is where you learn the most about who you are and what you're capable of.

Transferable Experience

Brooke has now played five concerts with Rocksteady. She's played different instruments, played with different people and faced the nerves several times. She's felt the enormous pride where everything goes exactly as planned, and also felt what it's like when things fall apart halfway through. She's benefited from the compound effect of learning. She's got experience.

And that experience is transferable. She's a regular face on the performing arts scene at school now, singing, dancing or doing all manner of things. Getting up in front of an audience doesn't faze her because she knows even if it doesn't quite go to plan, everything's going to be okay. That frees up her energy to be excited and focus on giving something amazing to her audience, whether she's playing in a rock band, has a speaking part at a school assembly or has to give a presentation to her class.

THE JOURNEY TO INDEPENDENCE

I'd like to finish the book by talking a bit about Rocksteady's general philosophies towards music education and where it's all heading. We teach children to play in bands and play concerts. They have fun, they build social skills, make new friends, and grow as people. They learn their notes and how to play them in time.

But once they've done that, where next?

With traditional music education the answer is fairly simple. Once you've passed your Grade 1, you move on to more challenging material with Grade 2. You then take Grades 3, 4, 5, 6, 7 and 8. You can do them in sequence or skip some, but either way you're progressing through increasingly challenging material.

Pop and rock music doesn't really work that way though.

The best songs aren't necessarily the hardest, and a lot of the music we enjoy today is remarkably simple by some standards. Improving in the art of composing catchy songs, playing with other people and entertaining your audience doesn't mean an increase in technical difficulty. To enforce such a structure in the children's learning would represent a big disconnection from what it's all about.

But lack of a technical drive doesn't mean that we don't focus on progression or that it isn't important. In Rocksteady progression is as important as in any other model of learning; we just have a slightly different view on what it means.

We've already covered at length the importance of enjoying whatever it is you do in this book. We've also covered building confidence through music. Once those two things are in place, the final piece in the progress puzzle is independence.

Awareness And Responsibility

Taj is ten years old. He has been playing guitar for eighteen months now and has played four different songs in four concerts. He knows where to find eight out of the twelve notes on the E string, can play power chords and is dabbling with a few open chords his teacher has been showing him.

Taj and his band have decided to learn 'The Man Who Can't

Be Moved' by The Script. The band leader Jason sets the context:

'Okay, so we've heard the song. The chords are G, A minor, D and C. How do we want to do this?'

Taj replies, 'I know where those notes are!'

'Excellent, so how are you going to play them in this song?'

'What do you mean?'

'Well, are you going to play the notes, open chords or power chords?'

'I think power chords would sound best.'

'Okay, let's try it with power chords.'

The band make their first attempt at the song with Taj playing power chords. The band leader then follows up.

'Cool. How did that sound?'

'Ummm, not too sure.'

The keyboard player Julia chimes in.

'Maybe they were a bit...loud.'

Jason continues the conversation.

'Okay, they are loud. Do we want them to be loud?'

Both Taj and Julia stop and consider this.

'I'd maybe like it to be loud in the chorus but not the verse,' says Taj.

'Yes, that would work!' says Julia.

'Alright, we're going to do power chords in the chorus. What are we going to do in the verse?'

'I could play single notes then. Should I play them high or low?'

'What do you think?'

'I'm not sure.'

'Okay, what's everyone else doing? What could you do that would fit in best with the band?'

Everyone looks blank.

'Shall we all play it again? Taj's job is to listen for where the space for him to play is.'

They all agree and play through the verse while Taj listens carefully.

'Well Julia is playing low, so maybe I could play a high part, but I'm not sure what I would play.'

'Okay, I'll show you,' says Jason.

He spends a minute showing Taj some higher versions of the same notes. Afterwards they all play the song together with the new higher notes.

Jason addresses the children again.

'Okay, how does it sound now?'

That certainly doesn't sound like teaching as we know it, so what's going on here? If you read back through the conversation you'll notice that Jason is spending most of his time asking questions rather than giving instructions. But not just any old questions: they're carefully chosen to raise Taj's awareness of what's going on around him and give him responsibility for the choices he's making.

Questions to raise awareness include 'How did that sound?' and 'What could you do that would fit in with the rest of the band?' By being asked these sort of open ended questions, the children are learning to consider what is going on around them and where they fit in. Rather than relying on their teacher to tell them it was great or to buck up their ideas, they're learning to think about it and make musical judgments for themselves.

Giving Taj responsibility is implicit in the way Jason conducts the questions. Even when Taj asks him directly 'What should I do?' about playing high or low notes, Jason doesn't give him instructions. He puts the ball back into Taj's court by giving him responsibility for listening and making the decision. Jason only steps in to instruct once Taj has taken responsibility and needs specific new skills to support his choice.

Taj has learned to consider his options given some basic information. He's learned to listen to what else is going on and consider his part in the greater whole. More importantly, he's felt responsibility for the choice he's making and has engaged in taking it seriously.

There's more to be considered: how many times should he play each note? Does it affect how the keyboard part sounds? Should he be playing them loudly, softly or a combination of the two? Could he be playing different notes altogether to create a harmony? If so, what's the best way to find those notes? Should he even be playing at all in the verse?

Awareness deepens. Responsibility increases. And awareness + responsibility = independence.

The Journey Of Learning

This may seem quite different from what you would imagine in a school lesson, and with good reason. In the early days of learning a new skill, be it music, maths or cross stitch, the quickest and most effective way to get started is to follow the instructions of someone who knows what they're doing. That's why we start with the simple and direct methods discussed in Chapter 5. This phase gives children the physical skills needed to perform well at their first concerts and build confidence.

However, if we continued this method for too long, our budding guitarist Taj would become dependent on his teacher telling him everything, including what to play and when to play it. When the teacher goes away, so does Taj's ability, because he's not aware of why each note is important and isn't learning to take responsibility for it. He simply knows that if he follows the instruction, he's told he's doing well. It's the fastest way to a result in the short term, but it won't give Taj independence, and we may see his enthusiasm and ability tailing off as he gets older and doesn't have the same stimulation around him.

A far better method for Taj's long term success is to foster his musical independence. We do this by shifting the focus away from raw physical skills and on to building awareness and responsibility around what he's playing. If he understands why it's a good idea to play a certain note, he can make similar choices in totally different situations. If he feels that he is responsible for his own learning, he can continue the journey himself and seek out the right role models, mentors and teachers as he goes. That way, music truly does become a skill for life. It's not dependent on his teacher, a sheet of music or needing to play the same songs. The journey can evolve as it goes, and Taj is in charge. It's his and nobody can take it away from him.

Given time, Taj will learn how to ask the right questions himself. This will be when he can learn independently. He'll have learned the ability to learn. He can follow instructions if he chooses to, but he also has the ability to write them. And that's a powerful place to be.

This can take many years to achieve and it somewhat mirrors the journey all children go through as they progress to adulthood. You start off life dependent on your parents for everything, from food and water to getting around. You're literally carried by your parents. Over time, you learn new skills, such as feeding yourself, communication, getting dressed, and getting yourself to school (if it's walkable).

After children have learned to take care of themselves to a basic extent, adults start to give them more freedom to make choices for themselves and guide them towards independence in this realm. This is the rocky road of teenage years for many.

Making decisions about your life can be a tricky thing to get right when you're still a beginner. It can be even harder if your parents, teachers or other responsible adults around you want to keep making those decisions for you. Still, it's a vital stage to navigate if you're to grow into an adult who can stand on their own two feet.

So if this stage usually comes about in teenage years, why are we attempting to build it with children much younger than that? Well, like most things, making decisions becomes a lot easier when you have experience of it. If they're done properly, music lessons can be a very safe environment to start practising the skill, and starting early pays big dividends further down the line. If a child enters their teenage years happy, confident and with the skills to take responsibility for their decisions then it's going to be a much smoother journey.

The Band That Ran Their Own Rehearsal

At the time of writing, the best expression we've seen of children making independent decisions is bands who run their own rehearsals. It's almost paradoxical to think of paying a music teacher to sit back and observe while the children get on with it, but to us, this is ultimately what we work towards. Much like you want to sit back and watch your children thrive as adults, we want to sit back and watch them be musicians.

Our resident tutor par excellence Richard recently took a Year 6 band called Steve's Wicked Enchanted Stuff through to their own performance of AC/DC's 'Back In Black'. He taught them the main parts, and then gave them the job of rehearsing it and putting the song together over four lessons leading up to their concert.

Richard explains: 'I've been teaching them since they were in Year 5, so nearly two years now. They seemed really keen to do the song. They were committed to it and had a lot of ideas, so I thought I'd let them run with it.

'I started by handing over half a lesson to them, and it went well so we took it from there. Two of them stepped up and took the lead, so there was a little bit of power play. They had to learn how to work together, but they were good enough friends to bow to each other occasionally.

'They had to overcome challenges. For example, they would get to the chorus, get stuck and then start the song over again, and it would take them a minute or so to get to the same mistake again. Learning the value of only repeating the tricky part was a good learning curve for them to follow.'

But they didn't just go from following Richard's instructions one day to running their own rehearsal overnight. It took time and focus.

'Once the ground rules and basics are established, I always set to pulling things out of people. Did that sound good? What can we do better?'

This band hardly needed any encouragement to do that, so it was a fairly short hop for them to go to 'How would you do it? What needs to be done?'

'They became very good at clarifying where they needed to make changes, how many times they had to play parts. One of the kids was constantly shouting "This is the fourth time!" over the music which other band members objected to, so we sat down at the end of that session and discussed non-verbal communication. We learned about eye contact so that they could communicate things subtly while playing.

'It was quite funny that they started using all my phrases to communicate with each other musically. It gave them an opportunity to understand why I was saying the things I was saying when they got to try them out themselves.'

Richard continues, 'It makes me sad to think that kids might just stop music. They often don't appreciate how good they really are. I love to think they'll carry on, even if not in the same band. With a bit of trial and effort they could put a band together themselves. If they're this awesome in Year 6, there's no reason not to continue, and if they've got the skills, then they're well on their way.'

And that's what it's all about at the end of the day. If the children leave each lesson happy, we've done half our job. If we manage to build their confidence, then we're 95% of the way there. If they have the skills they need to continue on their journey and be self-sufficient, then we've really achieved something.

'I Think It's Amazing, What I've Done.'

And that's exactly what we plan to do with Rocksteady: achieve something really special. Something special for music education as a whole, but also for every child we teach, because when you look underneath it all, that's why we do what we do.

It started out like so many of the best things in life: totally unplanned. We simply had the intention of delivering a better music education than we'd had at school. Through a combination of experience, experimentation and a whole lot of listening, we've created something that has the potential to change so many lives for the better.

I regularly speak to parents from all sorts of backgrounds, and they all tell me that they want their children to be happy, confident and to grow up to stand on their own two feet. That's exactly what we've built our company to help achieve, and while playing in a rock band may be a less conventional method of getting there, it's developed into an essential part of the school experience for many of the people we serve.

Playing in a band can be a relatively small part of some-one's life, or it can be huge. For those of us who work or teach for Rocksteady, it's become a fundamental part of who we are. For some of our previous pupils, it's gone on to define a big part of them, with their friendship groups, self-expression and creativity all being channelled into this art form. It's where they work out their frustrations, express love and pass the quiet times. For others it will merely be a stepping stone to something else.

I spoke to Shanaya from Chapter 1 after her last Rocksteady concert and she was clearly in a reflective mood on where music was going for her.

'I might like to teach music for some of the time, but really I love animals and would like to work in animal services.'

She paused thoughtfully.

'But I'm really happy that I've learned how to play and think it's amazing what I've done.'

I asked her what role music would play for her going forward.

'It will always be a hobby for me, because I know I can sit down at a keyboard and play and sing. I want to play in bands and make people happy, and I think I'll always be doing that.'

I'd watched Shanaya build in confidence, express herself, learn to connect better with others and channel her extremely determined mindset into music over the last four years. She'd grown as a musician certainly, but more importantly, she'd grown as a person. She was not as aware of those things as we were watching her, but she knows how they feel.

It can be summed up in much simpler terms: 'I'm happy and it's been amazing.'

And that's the essence of it. Whether it's the most important thing she ever does, a skill for the future or just a fun way to learn more about herself and the people around her, music has had an important part to play in her life, and I believe it can do the same for every child. It's our mission to make sure it reaches as many as possible.

AFTERWORD

Reaching as many children as possible...

I've said relatively little about Rocksteady's overarching mission until now because it's been all about the children. It's been about your child, or the group of children you're responsible for. They are at the heart of what we do, and it's them we focus on every day. But this ignores the fact that many people reading this book won't have access to our lessons yet as we're still a relatively young company (about the same age as most of the children we teach). We have a way to go to reach as many children as we can. But we're well on our way.

Over the last eight years we've grown from teaching a handful of children in a few schools to teaching thousands every week, and we're not planning on stopping any time soon. Like I said back in Chapter 3, if there is one Harry, there are millions. The truth of the matter is there are probably billions. The more positive, inspiring influences they have in their lives, the better, and it doesn't matter what the child's background is, the same thing can be said.

Every child needs a positive, safe space to grow into, and playing in a band is a great vehicle for this. Our mission is to empower as many children as possible, and we have a growing team in place (you can meet them on our website) who are working towards making that mission a reality. We've got a long way to go, but our sights are set very high indeed.

So how can you help? Well, the ideas in this book, like most things in life, will spread best through word of mouth, so you could tell other people about Rocksteady lessons, this book, or any of the messages in it. Share it, talk about it, give it to your friends. Follow us on social media, tweet about it. Tell us what you'd like to hear more about. Take the principles and apply them to other areas of educating and raising children. Visit www.rocksteadymusicschool.com and learn more about what we're up to. Follow our Band Of The Week competitions and give the children your support.

If you're a music teacher, why not try out some of the teaching methods yourself? Ask us for advice and let us know how you get on.

If you're a parent, a teacher, a politician or a business person and think you can help in any way, please get in touch.

The potential in children is limitless, and the potential of us all to make a difference for them is very real. Thank you for playing your part.

Here's to wherever the journey takes us next.

ACKNOWLEDGEMENTS AND THANKS

Rocksteady Music School wouldn't have got off the ground had it not been for the hard work and dedication of a whole host of people who have supported us in our journey so far.

My thanks go out to Mike Heelan and Nick Shaikh, who have been instrumental (pun intended) in the early growth stages of the company.

Ian Fellows for starting the journey with me and helping to get things off the ground.

All of the band leaders who have ever worked with us and given it their all. You've each taught us something important.

Richard Bushby, Matt Palmer, Mark Griffiths and Luke Hoey for the stories in this book and your continued dedication to doing great things every day.

Jessica Elliot and Ben Millier for being the supportive force behind the scenes, directly responsible for helping music reach thousands more children over the last few years.

Becky Hill for caring as much as you do and giving opportunities to experience music to so many children, including our Rocksteady bands. Your teaching brilliance is also the reason I chose to stick out traditional music education throughout primary school, without which Rocksteady wouldn't be here today.

David Richards for supporting my early guitar playing career and being open to whatever it was I wanted to learn.

Gordon Bull for being our teacher at a time when we needed it.

My wife Katherine for being my rock and supporting not just me, but the whole of Rocksteady whenever we need it.

Thank you to all of the schools and teachers who have supported us along the way, especially those who believed in what we were doing before there was any proof that it would work: Andy Richardson, Sam Hudson, Sue Wilson, Paul Walton, Liz Davies, Jon Reily, Liz Larcher, Jane Kent, Ruth Carty, Julie Luke.

To all the parents (including mine) who have supported their children through music over the years. Your support is what makes Rocksteady possible.

To Dianne Warren, Emma Beal, Paula Hanley, Dorothy Purkis, Melanie Hughes, Anna Gande and Amy Conway for contributing your stories and points of view.

To all the people who have helped in the preparation of this book. In addition to those mentioned above, David Horne, Libby Morgan, Scott Monks, Lucy McCarraher and Alison Jack for your feedback and valuable input on the various draft and editing stages.

And finally to the real stars of the show: all the children who have featured in this book, and also the many thousands more who have taught us so much over the years. The potential inside each and every one of you never ceases to inspire me.

THE AUTHOR

Mark Robinson is the founder of Rocksteady Music School, which teaches primary school children to play in bands. Music changed his life when he discovered rock music, playing the electric guitar and playing in bands as a child. He has spent his career so far providing the same opportunity to

thousands of other children in the South of the UK, and has plans to make the Rocksteady method available on a much bigger scale.

He's as passionate about teaching as he is about music, and believes that our goal in education should be to build the whole person, which includes children's confidence, happiness and independence. At the time of writing he has recently delegated the day to day running of Rocksteady Music School in order to focus on creating new companies in education and beyond.

You can learn more about Rocksteady Music School and get involved at www.rocksteadymusicschool.com

You can follow Mark's personal blog at www.marksremarks.com

Lightning Source UK Ltd.
Milton Keynes UK
UKHW04f1013181018
330761UK00003B/219/P